THE WAKE FOREST BOOK OF

Irish Women's Poetry

1967
2000

Selected and with a Preface by

Peggy O'Brien

Wake Forest University Press

WAKE FOREST UNIVERSITY PRESS
This book is for sale only in North America.
Copyright © Wake Forest University Press, 1999
Editor's Preface © Peggy O'Brien, 1999
All rights reserved.

For permission, required to reprint or broadcast
more than several lines, write to:
Wake Forest University Press
Post Office Box 7333, Winston-Salem, NC 27109

Book designed by Richard Eckersley
Printed in the United States by Thomson-Shore
Text set in Enschedé Trinité type
Library of Congress Catalogue Card 98-61874
ISBN 0-916390-88-8

Second printing, corrected and revised, 2003

The Wake Forest Book of Irish Women's Poetry, 1967–2000

This book is dedicated to my daughter,
Kristen Kennelly Murphy,
and my granddaughters,
Meg, Hannah and Grace Murphy –
my proud and personal
stake in Irish womanhood.

Contents

Eiléan Ní Chuilleanáin

Medbh McGuckian

Nuala Ní Dhomhnaill

Rita Ann Higgins

Paula Meehan

Moya Cannon

Mary O'Malley

Kerry Hardie

Editor's Preface

The poet Medbh McGuckian owns on the far northern coast of Country Antrim in the village of Ballycastle a small, stone house with a large, resonant history. Guglielmo Marconi, the famous Italian engineer, whose wife was Irish and mother half-Irish, once lived there. The first man to send a wireless message successfully across the span of the Atlantic, he spent his time in 1898 in that house bouncing electro-magnetic signals off nearby Rathlin Island rehearsing for the revolutionary event to follow. McGuckian gave her fourth, extremely enigmatic book of poems the title *Marconi's Cottage*, an appropriate choice for far more than personal reasons. A remarkable poet and, therefore, an inventor in her own right, she bravely experiments with language, discovering ways for it to deviate from the known, the accepted, and the predictable structures of meaning to demand a totally fresh hearing. Her voice on reception is probably not unlike that of the first radio communication: odd and yet our own, remote and yet immediate, in every way a miracle. The image of these other, parallel and pioneering waves, silent and invisible but audible on impact, dilating across a huge body of water, a whole ocean with its own tides and obscure depths, then finally finding a home in some distant, suddenly delighted listener's ear, can't but seem a metaphor for the different manifestations of female poetic energy contained here, its paradoxes and its trajectory. Transmission across the Atlantic, that well-worn but always new route for the Irish is, also, our confident aim for each of these poems.

When Seamus Heaney accepted the Nobel Prize for Literature in 1995, he generously asked his audience in Stockholm not just to honor him but to "think of the achievement of Irish poets and dramatists and novelists over the past forty years, among whom I am proud to count great friends." If the world hadn't known before then, after that it knew that poetry in Ireland is flourishing. It may still not know, however, the degree to which women have contributed to this prosperity. That is the primary reason for this book, to correct this partial perception, not just by presenting these poets as the world figures they intrinsically are, but by making it known how many there are. Eavan Boland seems to be the one Irish, female poet with an international, particularly American, reputation. Indisputably fine as she is, she is one of many equally fine but very different, in their separate ways less accessible, and lesser-known women poets. This volume, while including stunning newcomers and other poets of substantial worth, features the work of several mature poets of such incontrovertible and long-standing distinction, they must be counted among the artists responsible for the contemporary achievement Heaney marks. In addition to Boland, I am thinking specifically of Eiléan Ní Chuilleanáin, Medbh McGuckian, and Nuala Ní Dhomhnaill, who writes in Irish. For over thirty years, their work has not just participated in and consolidated this recent period of creativity, but, more important, has helped to direct this energy toward new forms of growth, ensuring that this spectacular flowering will continue and evolve. All the poets gathered here have, I believe, the capacity to exert this power over the writing of poetry beyond Ireland.

A glance at the Table of Contents reveals that unusually large numbers of poems, by the standards of most anthologies, have been garnered from the works of nine authors: Boland, Ní Chuilleanáin, McGuckian, Ní Dhomhnaill, Rita Ann Higgins, Paula Meehan, Mary O'Malley, Kerry Hardie, and Moya Cannon. Rather than epitomizing each poet by a few moments in her creative life, the predictable "anthology pieces," which can calcify a career in progress, these abundant selections allow the reader to hear each voice clearly in a range of registers and to grasp the scope of each poet's abiding concerns and development, then, if inclined, to make informed comparisons with the others. Reading in this way, deeply and broadly, should yield the paradox that the entanglement of all these poets in the underbrush of Irish culture is offset by the transcendent singularity of each.

Just as the inevitable but gradual attainment of pluralism in Ireland has begun to defeat the ambition, ironically pursued by diverse lobbyists, to put a single name on Irishness, so these poems subvert every preconception about what it means to be at once a woman and Irish, or even occasionally what it means to be a poem. Each of these voices is distinct and yet together they constitute a burgeoning of poetry that is distinctly Irish and female. This is not, however, to claim a separatist or essentialist endeavor by nature or design on behalf of gender or ethnicity. The achievement Heaney points to is the product of diverse voices, a legacy for poetry overall. The poets represented here influence their male contemporaries and are influenced by them. Ireland is too small and poetry too greedy to allow such clean binaries as men-and-women, Protestant-and-Catholic, to stand in practice. All the circles overlap; each remains a circle.

Take the perennial truth with regard to Ireland, that history has made its culture so complex as to be almost indecipherable. Compound that basic knowledge, rather helpful ignorance, by including the largely unrecorded experience of women and the ineffable privacies of a poem, thereby taking this as a caution to assume nothing beforehand about these poets. Each of these women, in common with men, inherits Ireland's history of serial invasion, plantation, and rebellion; the different repercussions are audible today on both sides of the Border: the muted but still rumbling "Troubles" in the North, the current economic boom in Europeanized Dublin. Yet, no two of these poets, as no two of their male counterparts, register these contingencies in the same way. No theory appears to me to be ultimately adequate to the mystery of a poem, and yet theory is of definite but discrete use in accounting for this extraordinary poetic fertility in Irish women, both its extent and its timing. Post-colonial theory goes some distance toward explaining the dramatic resurgence of literature after Yeats, thereby to some extent explaining these women. Also feminist theory can help to shape the story of how women come to find a voice; however, the historical silence of women in Ireland nests within the larger silence of a people. As theorists trained in feminism and post-colonialism have recognized, it is difficult to tease out fully the subtle interconnections and differences between these two forms of repression and release. The reasons for the layers of silence and their rupturings are surely many. Some may even

xvii

be factual, lying on the surface of history. They may have to do with the Catholic Church, its long tethering of women tightly to their fertility and family duties and now the relaxation of the Church's hold, as Ireland becomes more affluent and urban, as contraception and divorce, for instance, have become available. Finally, we must recognize accidental, human causes, like friendship, the potent force to which Heaney alludes. Many of the poets here are close friends, also with their male peers. Such mutual encouragement and, yes, rivalry, make a huge yet incalculable difference.

Furthermore, the politics of each poet here is inflected by individual concerns, be they of gender or class or ethnic identification. If anything, nationalist politics are the least in evidence. For some of these poets, at any one time, philosophy or religion or that more common but consuming passion, physical love, or, more simply still, being in the luminous natural world, may greatly overshadow but not necessarily eliminate politics, often the more pressing for remaining hidden. Like the male poets of roughly the same two generations – Heaney, John Montague, Thomas Kinsella, Derek Mahon, Michael Longley, Brendan Kennelly, Ciaran Carson, Paul Muldoon, to name the most prominent – these women are also responding to an enormous range of cultural forces with no set valency for each: religion, hence the Catholic Church as usual, for good and ill; history, not just Irish but British, European, and, given emigration, American history; literature, not just the richness of Irish oral culture, but English, American, Anglophone, and World Literature, especially European. But these women also participate in a women's history and culture both international and local. They are part of a literary lineage, slim but valued, on the Irish front that can be traced back to Eibhlín Dubh Ní Chonaill's searing elegy for her husband, slain by the British authorities. "The Lament for Art O'Leary" ("Caoineadh Airt Uí Laoghaire") written in Irish, is steeped both in the exclusive, feminine convention of the keen (caoineadh) and in a shared history: one dualism among many simultaneous truths to bear in mind.

In the North but also in the South, Irish poets face the predicament of balancing the uncompromising demands of poetry with the exigencies of politics. For Heaney, this means reconciling competing needs, for the liftoff of a true poem and the stability of staying grounded, of being true both to aesthetic, indeed spiritual, promptings and to moral responsibilities. While speaking for himself, particularly as a poet from highly politicized and suffering Northern Ireland, Heaney's broad outline of the problem applies to every poet here, all of whom find their own solutions, their unique equipoise. Some retain a more mimetic, thematic attachment to external reality; others, McGuckian in the forefront, take the autonomy of the poem, a potentially self-referential realm of play, to new lengths.

Patrick Kavanagh, that down-to-earth poet, whose brave, honest work inspired Montague, Kennelly, and Heaney to speak their own rural, Catholic, male beginnings has also been a beacon for women. Ní Chuilleanáin, one of the young poets who in the early sixties sat at Kavanagh's feet in the Dublin literary pub McDaid's, dedicated a book to the memory of his widow, Katherine. And Boland has praised Kavanagh's refusal to espouse the peasant stance thrust on him by the Literary Revival: "It was a costly and valuable resistance–exemplary to poets like myself who have come later, and with different purposes into that tradition." Kavanagh is the rough-and-ready defender of individualism, the freedom of the artist, especially from the tyranny of having to look and sound Irish. A cussedly contrary poet, he is rooted in the local, touts the parochial, yet insists on inheriting the earth when it comes to his art. It is this independence and rightful sense of entitlement above all that set this later half-century of Irish literature off from the previous, more self-conscious first half of the "Irish Renaissance." Witness the cultural eclecticism, say, of Muldoon or Ní Chuilleanáin's immersion in Europe. The women collected here are the equal inheritors of this newfound self-confidence and legitimate license to experiment, to pick and choose among influences and subjects and styles.

Kavanagh in his groundbreaking, long poem, "The Great Hunger," which exposed Ireland in the 1930's for its material and spiritual poverty, attacks absolutism as the enemy of fulfillment. He points to a loss of crucial nonchalance in not "picking up life's truths singly," but instead longing only for "the Absolute envased bouquet." He regards this absolutism as a dire error, the fatal flaw jointly of an overly metaphysical Irish Catholicism and the isolationism of Ireland just after Independence. Absolutism is anathema to poetry. It is also lethal to good literary interpretation or, for that matter, sound cultural history.

No two women presented here adopt the same political or formal strategies for life or poetry. They come from various classes, different parts of Ireland, individual families, are married or not, have children or don't, are of different ages, have come under different poetic influences, simply have different temperaments, above all different imaginations. Most have traveled, given readings, even lived in other countries. Variety and similarity will be observed at every turn. All these poems come out of a context determined by history and gender and class, yet each of them on close inspection, like a magic pellet dropped into water, begins to differentiate, fill out, assume strange life, surprise, become a poem.

The failure of patriarchy to render by means of flat reason the round world in which women live is a common feminist theme, and maps have become a common metaphor to illustrate this misrepresentation. Three poems here appeal to this theme, employ this metaphor but, tellingly, each does so to different effect. Kerry Hardie, in "We Change the Map," the first poem of her first collection, makes a plea for the chosen enclosure of domestic life, eschewing the overview a map presumes. Rita Ann Higgins in "Remapping the Borders" charts an experience that threatens her habitual sexual definition. At a conference in Texas, a homoerotic moment takes her by surprise: "Me, thigh, knee, no / I saw nothing." The idea of seeing nothing, the denials upon which civilization is predicated, becomes Boland's theme in "That the Science of Cartography is Limited." But as the disquisitional title predicts, this poem, driven by a philosophical purpose, uses the gender of the viewer finally to address matters of universal, epistemological import: the limits of linear, historical narrative to contain the infinite ramifications of tragedy, the failure of language to communicate the silence of great loss. Referring to a now overgrown road that was constructed as famine relief work and ended where the starving builders died, Boland reminds herself, more than us, that she studies maps to be chastened, particularly as a poet. Her faith is in words, as the surveyor trusts his theodolite, but it can't map death anymore than words can. The road "will not be there."

The appalling hush of that concluding negation includes the silencing of the language those men in that earlier time were speaking: Irish. It too was one of the fatalities of the Great Famine, or nearly. All these poets in some way register the mute pressure of this absence; but, as with Irish artists since Joyce, this loss may be turned to the poet's advantage, heightening an already intense engagement with language. For women, an added degree of alienation and intensification, a double disenfranchisement, may result in an extra determination to put one's own signature on the language. Such reclamation through innovation is, however, also the hallmark of Muldoon's and Ciaran Carson's work; and McGuckian's preeminence in this respect may have as much to do with her Belfast connections as her femaleness, or Irishness, or genius. What is more, there is little romanticizing about and a great deal of hard commitment to the Irish language. Any anxiety about its peril is undercut by a sober reminder of the still lingering punitiveness of the language movement under the nationalist program after Independence. Notwithstanding and, no doubt, because of this charged ambivalence about two languages, all poetry coming out of Ireland today, male or female, to some degree is born out of a bilingual, creative environment. The range of accommodation to bilingualism stretches from the easy coexistence of poetry purely in Irish and purely in English; to poetry which, like that of Ní Chuilleanáin, Muldoon, and Carson, is studded with bits of untranslated Irish, whole phrases, and covert puns for the initiated; to poetry, as ever, influenced by recent or past Irish poems; to whole careers, like Michael Hartnett's, that move in and out of the two languages with fluency; to poetry that more abstractly questions the primacy of English to a degree only possible in a culture with a racial memory of another complete and resonant linguistic past.

In recognition of this hybrid reality, we have undertaken what at first may seem an indulgence: Nuala Ní Dhomhnaill's poems appear both in the Irish originals and their English translations. This is not just the only conscionable way to treat a major poet, or a proportionate recognition of Ní Dhomhnaill's central place in Irish poetry overall, regardless of gender. It is also a symbolic indication of the importance of the Irish language and its literature to contemporary Irish poetry in general. The list of Ní Dhomhnaill's translators reads like an index of the best of living Irish poets. She has been especially lucky in finding Muldoon, whose imagination seems so wedded to hers that his translations are fully realized poems with the immediacy and transparency of originals. This collaboration alone points to the vital interplay between both languages now.

The fact is, however, that all true poems as they negotiate the treacherous gap between inspiration and execution are translations. The heightened danger for Irish women is that no language, Irish or English, has until now been fully tested to tell their story. Like Patrick Kavanagh, whom Heaney describes as having "wrested his idiom bare-handed out of a literary nowhere," these poets have had to master a free fall. In fairness, however, the situation for women has not been as stark as that Kavanagh faced. Two earlier, still living, women poets not included here, since strict contemporaneity gives, I hope, this volume its edge, must be accorded their due as precursors. I speak of Maire Mhac An tSaoi, a poet in Irish, and Eithne Strong, who writes in both languages. Ní Chuilleanáin, a Renaissance scholar whose sensuous, mysterious, historically removed poems have a Keatsian opulence and finish to them, openly acknowledges her debt to Mhac An tSaoi, a poet of spare lyricism and a repository of erudition about ancient Ireland. Strong, with her exuberant nonconformity, provides an inheritance not just or primarily for Ní Dhomhnaill and her sister poets in Irish, but for all who have made permeable the membrane between poetry publication in Irish and English. Furthermore, it is purely for want of enough good translations that Biddy Jenkinson, Caitlín Maude, and Áine Ní Ghlinn, all poets in Irish, were not considered for inclusion.

An even more oblique connection between the Irish tradition and a poet in English is found in the revolutionary poetry of Medbh McGuckian, the most daring and innovative poet in this volume. McGuckian's female content, with its synchronic perceptions and heightened sensuality, is so resistant to ordinary language, it would appear that she has been pressured from within, like Gerard Manley Hopkins, to forge a radically revised poetry, one in her case that flouts conventional syntax, proliferates ellipses, makes illogicality the only certainty. Not gratuitously obscure, she occasionally tries to translate herself, as in "Prie-Dieu" confessing, "This oblique trance is my natural / Way of speaking," or in "The Partner's Desk" where she refers, with Joycean point and wit, to her deliberately foreign speech as "my un-English language."

Finally, all of these poems, like all Irish literature in English, deploy a more or less hybrid dialect, Hiberno-English. It is not just a matter of inserting the odd Irish word, as Mary O'Malley does in "Liadan with a Mortgage Briefly Tastes the Stars," where her mythological heroine goes "*stravaiging* among the planets," but of imperceptibly transposing Irish grammar into English, which encourages a wordplay and authenticity crucial for poetry. Making matters even more complicated, Ní Chuilleanáin, who bears an Irish name but writes in English, often assumes a cosmopolitan, even polyglot voice that directly challenges monolingualism. The adaptable, capable women in Ní Chuilleanáin's poems, often nuns serving on the continent, tend to speak a second or third language, French, maybe Italian. The youngest poet included here, Moya Cannon, who writes cool, elegant poems, each one like a bleached bone, has a philological zeal reminiscent of an earlier Heaney, a polished brevity akin to Longley's. She holds and handles individual words as though they were fascinating, exotic objects, as in "Thole-Pin," an entire poem about the survival of a word, aptly "thole," "to endure." That the chosen word is of Old Norse affiliation but of no ultimately identifiable origin is also appropriate given the poet's affiliation with a culture where searching for linguistic purity can seem pure folly, counter to the power of survival wondered at by her poem. The inserted anglicisms in Ní Dhomhnaill's Irish poems contribute to their up-to-the-minute, hip irreverence and iconoclasm.

All these poets delight in language, revivify it, put it to fresh tasks. McGuckian has an astonishing vocabulary. Her head, for instance, is a positive *florilegium*, a lexicon of every flower's name carefully folded between the pages of her compendious imagination. Ní Chuilleanáin dusts off arcane, even antique words, making them shine. Take her opening to the "Pig-boy," a disturbingly erotic, violent poem straight from the cellar of the subconscious: "It was his bag of tricks she wanted, surely not him: / The pipkin that sat on the flame, its emissions." The witty onomatopoeia of *pipkin* must have set this poem ticking. I am assured by those with a command of Irish that Ní Dhomhnaill's poems expand the language itself, so agile and mischievous is she, so perfect is her pitch. Ní Dhomhnaill's work gives another meaning to the term "mother tongue."

This acute self-consciousness about language is ground zero for any poet but especially those whose ethnicity and gender add further pressure, and energy, to their relationship with words. These poets may fetishize language, but they also use it for the urgent purpose of expressing the uniqueness of their lives, a vast range of experience, only some of it openly involved with Ireland. The face of Ireland may be hardly recognizable in many of these poems, except perhaps in a tiny, telling turn of phrase or a fleeting, indigenous image. Boland, the most overtly political of these poets in relation to gender and the nation, writes her best poem, an impeccable poem in my estimation, "The Black Fan My Mother Gave Me," about flirtation, not only its dangers, but also the art and beauty in these controlled but sudden unfoldings of desire. There are, however, frequent glimpses of the Irish landscape, from the opalescent stone and aqueous skies of Connemara in O'Malley to the Dublin Mountains and the river Liffey in Boland. In contrast there are Higgins' grim housing estates outside Galway City; and McGuckian's fantasized, aristocratic interiors, a cross between a chateau and a dacha; and Ní Chuilleanáin's story book towers and tapestried chambers and subterranean kitchens where phantasmagorias occur. That said, however, many of these women, like their male counterparts, have also tried to untangle in their own terms the major knots in Irish history: McGuckian's latest book, a book-length poem, *Shelmalier*, centers around the 1798 rebellion.

Also the influence of Europe, the chosen asylum of the Wild Geese and expatriate, Irish writers for generations, is here. McGuckian's reverence for Rilke can be felt in almost every

breathless, visionary line, likewise, further afield, for
Mendelstam and Tsvetaesva. Like other Irish poets such as the
modernist 30's poet, Denis Devlin, Ní Chuilleanáin draws
habitually on Ireland's historic, Catholic connection with the
continent. Less out of fervor than perhaps an intellectual, ur-
bane faith and a fascination with hagiography, she has given us
a clutch of poems with saints in their titles, such as "St Mary
Magdalene Preaching at Marseilles" and "St Margaret of Cor-
tona." Ní Chuilleanáin is drawn to the place women occupy
in the lives of the saints, the mystical, erotic, self-immolating,
but self-possessing states of mind their examples offer and
the way these lives dovetail with everyday martyrdoms and dis-
plays of courage.

   Not all of the poets here, however, have such attenuated
spiritual and aesthetic sensibilities. And some don't give a toss
apparently for the idea of the nation. Their concerns are more
quotidian, their poems born out of unvarnished daily living.
Hardie writes such poems; so does Paula Meehan. Many are
generated by compassion or outrage, a sense of injustice, indig-
nation at the ways power is used against women, the poor, and
children, and combinations thereof. Ní Chuilleanáin's harrow-
ing, discretely indirect, "Chrissie" is, I think, a poem about
rape. And Higgins has written with frightening terseness about
incest in "Philomena's Revenge" and domestic abuse in
"She is Not Afraid of Burglars." Other poems confess to the
guilt and ambivalence of the female writer in relation to other
women, especially mothers and sisters. Meehan's minor mas-
terpiece, "The Pattern," is a simple, clear unflinching portrait of
her working-class mother and the guilty rebellion of a poet-
daughter. Some poems identify the poet with the worker, even
the downtrodden, and question the elitism of creative work.
Those all too familiar, female sounds of self-doubt, fears about
professional fraudulence, also sadly abound. Yet, in "Consump-
tive in the Library" Higgins comically exposes the unease with
which the self-aggrandizing mantle of poet can weigh on fe-
male shoulders. McGuckian in her "Elegy for an Irish Speaker"
imagines her recently dead father speaking "so with my con-
sciousness / and not with words, he's in danger / of becoming a
poetess": feminized, trivialized, no longer her powerful father.

For O'Malley these painful issues of gender, ethnicity, and class often swirl together in a turbid pool of rage and shame and pride. A small but powerful poem, "The Visitor," captures the simultaneous impact of all these forces in one burning moment of a Connemara girl's life, being presented by her mother to an English male visitor. The child feels branded by her "homemade dress" and "misshapen accent." A number of poems here deal with that perennial, female problem of prizing the self free from the warped image presumed to be imposed on it by the perceiver, usually male. Mirroring is ubiquitous. The most indelible instance may appear in Ní Chuilleanáin's "London," where the poet recalls talking in a pub to a friend who has just had a mastectomy. Sitting there amidst a lunchtime crowd of men, the poet notices the friend's peripheral vision fixing on a shiny metal urn, convex as a breast and cruelly reflecting back the fact of perhaps imminent death. For her part, Ní Chuilleanáin regularly resists being gazed at by intently looking back. She is the supreme observer, quiet, penetrating, but also humble, always looking at a steep, personal angle, often plural, deliberately destabilizing angles. Her searching, lambent intelligence investigates but never exhausts the darkness it nonetheless penetrates.

The politics of the male gaze is Boland's compelling theme. Take, for example, "Degas's Laundresses," where the female poet inserts herself both behind the artist's gaze to expose his lust and greed and in front to intercede for the working-class women he's coldly depicting, to identify with their labor, their helpless exposure. Boland also is credited with translating this form of appropriation into Irish nationalist terms. In her early essay, "A Kind of Scar," she articulated a truth that provided the ideological springboard for her career. Boland observes there that Irish women have been doubly colonized: first, with Irish men, by numerous foreign invasions and, second, exclusively as women, by nationalism, a male preserve. As an icon of the long-suffering nation, the Irish woman becomes "Mother Ireland," a static and silent object distanced from her actual, decidedly unromantic self. Boland has in reaction taken a documentary interest in the daily lives of women and modeled her poetic persona as a wife and mother in the suburbs according to these dictates.

Righting with fiery humor the wrong that Boland dissects,

Ní Dhomhnaill in "Cathleen" gives a latter day Kathleen Ní Houlihan a thing or two to say about her former life as Mother Ireland: "even if every slubberdegullion once had a dream-vision / in which she appeared as his own true lover, those days are just as truly over." The term "dream-vision" is an allusion to a convention of Irish traditional poetry, the *aisling*, which features the sudden revelation of a dazzling, idealized woman who is Ireland. Parodic *aislings* are a regular feature of contemporary Irish poetry, like Muldoon's jaundiced "Aisling" where his dream woman has a sexually transmitted disease, and Ní Dhomhnaill's "Nude," included here, where a fine figure of a man is objectified and visually stripped in benign revenge by frankly appreciative, female eyes (the translation piquantly by Muldoon). Time and again Ní Dhomhnaill takes lusty advantage of the precedent for female sexual candor in traditional Irish poetry, as in Brian Merriman's "The Midnight Court" ("*Cúirt an Mheán Oíche*"). Less optimistically, there's Meehan's chilling "Zugzwang," where a marriage break-up is rendered in terms of the male gaze that never stopped dominating it. In the end the wife's self-image is apocalyptically shattered. Boland's "Achill Woman" also tries to subvert the *aisling* but may, in fact, reenact the appropriation of the male gaze by the female poet's mythologizing of a less privileged woman. Notwithstanding this irony, the feat of breaking free of the petrifaction inherent in being a muse and not a poet appears over and over as a theme, never more successfully than in Ní Chuilleanáin's "Pygmalion's Image." Here this miraculous birth of authentic speech is presented as literally earth shaking: "Everything the scoop of the valley contains begins to move / . . . A green leaf of language comes twisting out of her mouth."

Bold, innovative solutions to poetic, personal, and historical stasis are displayed throughout this volume. Meehan in her delicate elegy "Child Burial" exploits to new effect, as Ní Dhomhnaill has done, the traditional convention, apparent in the charming scribbles of animals in the margins of The Book of Kells, of using nature imagery to carry emotion. Meehan addresses the dead child, poignantly giving him warm, tiny life again, as "my lamb, my calf, my eaglet, / my cub, my kid, my nestling." In the vanguard with this revisionist strategy, Ní

Dhomhnaill, irreverent and learned, uses the magic taken for granted in oral culture to express the transmogrifications which are everyday in a contemporary woman's life. The ploy has the effortless imprimatur of history, since Irish storytelling enjoys a powerful female pedigree, Peig Sayers, the renowned Blasket Island storyteller, being just one exponent. Ní Dhomhnaill in "The Battering" utilizes the oral tradition's accommodations of extreme, even dissociated, feelings and actions performed under duress by assigning them to supernatural agents like the Fairies. Irish folklore, a proper inheritance, enables Ní Dhomhnaill to traverse a vast and challenging psychological terrain beyond the bounds of confessionalism. Similarly Ní Chuilleanáin, whose moonlit poems have the chiaroscuro feel of the Brothers Grimm, rarely relies on naked disclosure.

All this creative activity is part of a dynamic process of self-representation, for which confessionalism would not only be, for the most part, inappropriate, given the ingrown closeness of Irish society, but also inadequate to the task. Poets proverbially search for a voice, but in Ní Chuilleanáin's "J'ai Mal à nos Dents," where an elderly, Franciscan nun, who has lived her adult life in France and always juggled two languages, finally comes home to silence: "They handed her back her body, / Its voices and its death." One voice may not be sufficient for a woman with many roles, many lives. Similarly no prescription for identity or poetry works for any of these poets. Take the issue of myth, the question of whether centuries of male inscription have placed myth out of bounds for women. Boland, who in "Making Up" states bluntly "myths are made by men," has been instructed in this matter by Adrienne Rich's poem "Diving into the Wreck." Wary of myth, Boland dares to reinvent it in her wrenching poem about her daughter, "The Pomegranate," based on the story of Demeter and Persephone; whereas Ní Chuilleanáin, as in "The Second Voyage" about Odysseus, often strides without a qualm into the catacombs of myth, a haunted space, ideally suited for her allegorical imagination.

Similarly, Catholicism is both exposed for the damage the Church has done to women and tapped for the legacy of spiritual and artistic richness it bestows. O'Malley in "Cealetrach" tries to imagine the pain of all those women who had to bury their unbaptized infants in unconsecrated ground. Ní Dhomhnaill's anti-clerical "Miraculous Grass" excoriates a sexually active, hypocritical priesthood for demonizing the ultimately inviolable sexuality of women. Ní Chuilleanáin's new poem "Translation (for the reburial of the Magdalens)" pays homage to the scores of young, unmarried mothers who spent entire, virtually imprisoned, lifetimes working and living in laundries run, appropriately, by the Magdalen nuns. On the other hand, one of Ní Chuilleanáin's most wondrous poems, "Fireman's Lift," a structurally complex work, which telescopes an early memory of looking up at a mural of the Virgin Mary through her mother's eyes into a later, analogous view, makes maternal love the principle of creation itself: of the world and art, the poet and the poem. The later instance of total empathy on the poet's part occurs when the mother is near death and looking up again, but this time into the faces of those who are supporting her in a fireman's lift. Ní Chuilleanáin has said that her first attraction to Corregio's rendering of the Assumption on the cupola of the cathedral in Parma was the palpable weight of the woman paradoxically becoming weightless. In grounding one of the most disembodying projections of patriarchy, the Virgin Mary born of an Immaculate Conception, in the body, Ní Chuilleanáin challenges the very core of Judea-Christian, western values that emanate from an idealization of the mother. She strikes a double but not contradictory political posture as someone both Irish and female: celebrating the glories of the once threatened religion of the majority in Ireland but also revising the Church's limiting discourse about women by reinvesting in it. Self-possessed rather than iconoclastic, Ní Chuilleanáin in "Fireman's Lift" rewrites the myth of maternity from a daughter's perspective, making her mother both the awe-inspiring other and her own flesh. This architectural poem which carries massive implications is buoyed by a mature, female subjectivity: autonomous because it's unafraid to be contiguous with another, to love.

The body is the democratic reality that binds all these poets, however refracted corporeality may be by widely ranging relationships to it. Boland in "Making Up" shows how a woman can be so in thrall to the male gaze, so collusive that she makes an artifact of her own flesh. For McGuckian, the body is the fulcrum of her entire enterprise. She writes a female erotic, overturning centuries of male speculation about women. Far from flattening identity through this wearing of an exaggeratedly feminine mask, McGuckian, who habitually, like a child playing dress-up, dons elaborate costumes, flirts with other lives, manages to further complicate gender, as in "The Aphrodisiac" where she inserts the impish indecision of whether her persona once "would dress in pink taffeta, and drive / A blue phaeton, or in blue, and drive / a pink one." McGuckian is well capable of striking a masculine pose, particularly when she finds herself wrapped in a somber, as she wittily puts it, "cardiganed" mood, that effaces her femininity. The first principle of her gynocentric universe is to favor ambiguity. Her only half tongue-in-cheek opening to "From the Dressing Room" makes this clear: "Left to itself, they say, every foetus / Would turn female, staving in, nature / Siding then with the enemy that / Delicately mixes up genders." In "The Moon Pond" she pulls the reader into herself, a uterine space which again is the source of literal creation, a chamber of hitherto complete darkness and silence which the poet sets resonating. Her language is both unfamiliar to the reader and vaguely remembered, with a provenance, perhaps, in a past life, a foreign but first-known space. This speech has a phenomenological feel, as though skin could talk.

   Almost all of McGuckian's poems occur within confined spaces, rooms, her house, her walled garden, and many of these domains are extended metaphors of the body, a similar kind of immurement as that provided by Ní Chuilleanáin's convents and towers. The problems for autonomy which this immersion in anatomy creates is one of McGuckian's recurring themes, surfacing with poignancy in interviews. On one occasion she exclaimed: "Being a woman is so incredibly difficult. And being a woman poet, it's a contradiction in terms. A woman is so naturally fluid and her mind is so dominated by her body, that for a woman to write real poetry – as men have been able to do – is difficult." Once more, "The Fascination of What's Difficult," of everything that might kill poetry, becomes a necessary precondition for its life. Every poem becomes a triumph over the abyss that immediately precedes and births it. Ní Chuilleanáin also dips into a fluid, subconscious world in poems that often literally feature water as their major element, such as "River with Boats" and "The Water Journey." Boland, in "The Journey" has Sappho speak of "the silences in which are our beginnings, / in which we have an origin like water." Finally Cannon, the most purely metaphysical poet here, who filters her engagement with the body through her cerebrality, for example in "Crannog," probes the universal and numinous attraction of water. The actual locus of her attention, a prehistoric, pagan lake-dwelling in the Irish midlands, recalls a human being's origins as a fetus in the womb, "a dry island and a fort / with a whole lake for a moat." As Cannon simply states, "much of us longs to live in water."

This life-giving tension between containment and flux is echoed on every level in these poems, not least by the equilibrium between form and content. While there are notable exceptions, for example, occasional forays into free verse, the majority of these poems cleave to form, if not formalism. Stanzas for the most part are constant, as are lines of even length, or even weight. It is within these confines that new life appears arising out of language whose fluid, even gravity defying, properties are discovered by a variety of traditional poetic devices put to radical use. The audacious inventiveness and orthodox mastery these poets display make them invaluable examples for all artists trying to assert their individuality within certain cultural givens, especially the bastion of poetic precedent. They may even answer at their most sublime moments the proverbial question asked by the artist in Ireland from Yeats to Mahon and Muldoon, of whether poetry matters. Many readers regard McGuckian as an utterly inscrutable, irremediably hermetic poet. The more astute, I believe, see her as an ontological poet of immeasurable impact. For her handling of time alone, collapsing all major events, birth, orgasm, and death into the all consuming moment of each, absorbing time into a woman's space, she can alter one's understanding of history, the temporal narratives that support politics, especially in Ireland.

xxxi

The poets represented here are those who are included in the national conversation about poetry. They are the ever echoing, frequently envy-inducing voices in other poets' heads, be they male or female. This is not to say, however, that this book doesn't leave out poets of exceptional promise and undeniable accomplishment who some day soon may require a reconsidering of these choices, since this is a process and change can be swift. I'm thinking of Eva Bourke, Katie Donovan, Mary Dorcey, Vona Groarke, Joan McBreen, Katherine Phil MacCarthy, Sinéad Morissey, Joan Newman, Mary O'Donnell and Enda Wiley. No doubt too there will be other names we don't know yet, not always of young women but of new poets. In deference to the established fact that the muse can descend on a woman at any moment, the poets I have chosen are arranged not according to when they were born but when they became widely heard.

To invoke the etymological association of flowers with the word anthology in a preface to one may by now be a cliché; but since these are poets of proven subversion and affirmation, I'll presume to use the conceit with freshness. One must never forget the power of one true poem not only to change the landscape of poetry but to explode, like William Carlos William's "saxifrage . . . that splits the rocks," our previous constructions of reality, gender included. I see this book as a glorious, fragrant bouquet, neither, God forbid, Kavanagh's "Absolute envased" one, nor a glass specimen case which inventories every flower in the field. The poems carefully picked and gathered here in generous armfuls are among the most splendid blooms I know in Irish poetry, any poetry, and hardy too. I hope the reader will not hesitate to rub them up against each other, asking questions about women and Irish culture and poetry itself, making the nap on their petals rise. They will not bruise easily. Above all, I hope the reader will simply accept these poems, as I do, as a gift.

PEGGY O'BRIEN

ACKNOWLEDGMENTS

I want to thank many people for their help throughout the process of producing this anthology, work that took place in various stages on both sides of the Atlantic. First, the people in Winston-Salem. Without Dillon Johnston's belief in the need for such a volume, it would not exist. For his long-standing devotion to and vast knowledge of Irish poetry, and for the tact, patience, sensitivity, and respect he showed me from beginning to end, I thank him. And his wife, Guinn Batten, for the unselfish gift of her time and sophistication as a reader. And emphatically, Candide Jones, the manager of the Wake Forest University Press, whose high spirits, hard work, and publishing savvy saw us through the long haul of making an idea a reality. Also at the Press, Carter Smith and Betsy Phillips. Finally, Richard Eckersley, our designer and an artist, for the physical beauty of this book.

Equally, were it not for my many friends and colleagues in Ireland, this book would not have had a chance. I thank Theo Dorgan and his staff for making the resources of Poetry Ireland completely available to me. Above all, Harriet O'Donovan Sheehy, my dear friend and second mother, both for her wisdom and for providing a second home for me, a perch high on a hill overlooking Dalkey Island. Doubly blessed with physical perspectives from which to regard many, many poems, I was lent by Paul Wojcik and Emma Stewart-Liberty their pristine home as a study, allowing me to read slim volumes looking out a floor-to-ceiling window on the Irish Sea. And Maureen Tatlow, who knows me, found just the right words always to spur me on when I tended to flag. Also Luke Gibbons, whose encyclopedic knowledge of Irish culture made him indispensable when it came to compiling the annotations. Finally, for myriad, infinite kindnesses, Anne and Peter Kelly, Mary Ellen Fox, Adrienne Fleming, and Tony Glavin.

More immediately, I owe a debt of gratitude to an array of people in western Massachusetts. To Jim Kelly in the University of Massachusetts, Amherst, Library for his inestimable, expert assistance with bibliographical work. Also, for rushing to my aid with solutions to documentation problems, I thank both

Jack Harrison of the University of Massachusetts Press and my former graduate assistant, Maureen Fielding. Mary Irwin kept me sane during bouts of panic over deadlines by means of her sublime calm and rare capacity to listen. Also, as a professional, she supplied translations from Irish and French. Mary Jo Salter gave me actual tea and substantial sympathy, in addition to the benefit of her experience as a poet and an editor. Brad Leithauser, who knows everything, helped to lever the most recondite references. Laura Doyle, of the University of Massachusetts English Department, in directing my thinking toward the theoretical contexts in which this poetry can be considered, gently opened my mind to new ways of understanding what I thought I knew. Also in my department, I must particularly thank Deborah Carlin, Stephen Clingman, Margo Culley, Anne Herrington, and Kathleen Swaim, for succeeding in creating the professional conditions in which this work could be done. As well, Doris Newton, Deborah Dargis, Donna Johnson, and Meg Caulmare for their unstinting clerical help.

In Washington, D.C., Kate Slattery of the Irish Embassy provided the kind of insights about the Irish language tradition that only a fluent speaker can. Also from Washington, Joseph Hassett, an independent scholar of Irish poetry, lent his encouragement at a critical juncture. And in New York City, Julie Pratt Shattuck, who speaks in poems, was and is an inspiration.

It goes without saying that I can never thank adequately all the poets in this book simply for their poems and many for their friendship, the innumerable, unplanned, wandering conversations that have given their work and that of others an intimate habitation in my mind. Needless to say, a number of Irish male poets have also contributed to this pleasurable education, and when it came to this book were staunch in their support.

Finally, I could not have done this work without the joyful companionship of Wynn Abranovic, all our restorative walks in the woods and fields of Amherst, our leisurely meals, overall the peace, affection, good sense, care, and droll humor he bestows on me daily.

The Wake Forest Book of Irish Women's Poetry, 1967–2000

Eavan Boland

New Territory

Several things announced the fact to us:
The captain's Spanish tears
Falling like doubloons in the headstrong light
And then of course the fuss –
The crew jostling and interspersing cheers
With wagers. Overnight
As we went down to our cabins, nursing the last
Of the grog, talking as usual of conquest,
Land hove into sight.

Frail compasses and trenchant constellations
Brought us as far as this.
And now air and water, fire and earth
Stand at their given stations
Out there are ready to replace
This single desperate width
Of ocean.
         Why do we hesitate?
                 Water and air
And fire and earth, and therefore life, are here.
And therefore death.

Out of the dark man comes to life and into it
He goes and loves and dies
(His element being the dark and not the light of day,)
So the ambitious wit
Of poets and exploring ships have been his eyes –
Riding the dark for joy –
And so Isaiah of the sacred text is eagle-eyed because
By peering down the unlit centuries
He glimpsed the holy boy.

Making Up

My naked face;
I wake to it.
How it's dulsed and shrouded!
It's a cloud,

a dull pre-dawn.
But I'll soon
see to that,
I push the blusher up,

I raddle
and I prink,
pinking bone
till my eyes

are
a rouge-washed
flush on water.
Now the base

pales and wastes.
Light thins
from ear to chin,
whitening in

the ocean shine
mirror set
of my eyes
that I fledge

in old darks.
I grease and full
my mouth.
It won't stay shut:

I look
in the glass.
My face is made,
it says:

Take nothing, nothing
at its face value:
Legendary seas,
nakedness,

that up and stuck
lassitude
of thigh and buttock
that they prayed to –

it's a trick.
Myths
are made by men.
The truth of this

wave-raiding
sea-heaving
made up
tale

of a face
from the source
of the morning
is my own:

Mine are the rouge pots,
the hot pinks,
the fledged
and edgy mix
of light and water
out of which
I dawn.

Degas's Laundresses

You rise, you dawn
roll-sleeved Aphrodites,
out of a camisole brine,
a linen pit of stitches,
silking the fitted sheets
away from you like waves.

You seam dreams in the folds
of wash from which freshes
the whiff and reach of fields
where it bleached and stiffened.
Your chat's sabbatical:
brides, wedding outfits,

a pleasure of leisured women
are sweated into the folds,
the neat heaps of linen.
Now the drag of the clasp.
Your wrists basket your waist.
You round to the square weight.

Wait. There behind you.
A man. There behind you.
Whatever you do don't turn.
Why is he watching you?
Whatever you do don't turn.
Whatever you do don't turn.

See he takes his ease
staking his easel so,
slowly sharpening charcoal,
closing his eyes just so,
slowly smiling as if
so slowly he is

unbandaging his mind.
Surely a good laundress
would understand its twists
its white turns,
its blind designs –

it's your winding sheet.

Woman in Kitchen

Breakfast over, islanded by noise,
she watches the machines go fast and slow.
She stands among them as they shake the house.
They move. Their destination is specific.
She has nowhere definite to go:
she might be a pedestrian in traffic.

White surfaces retract. White
sideboards light the white of walls.
Cups wink white in their saucers.
The light of day bleaches as it falls
on cups and sideboards. She could use
the room to tap with if she lost her sight.

Machines jigsaw everything she knows.
And she is everywhere among their furor:
the tropic of the dryer tumbling clothes.
The round lunar window of the washer.
The kettle in the toaster is a kingfisher
swooping for trout above the river's mirror.

The wash done, the kettle boiled, the sheets
spun and clean, the dryer stops dead.
The silence is a death. It starts to bury
the room in white spaces. She turns to spread
a cloth on the board and irons sheets
in a room white and quiet as a mortuary.

7

bag,
the seed.

Slap
the flanks back.
Flatten

paps.
Make finny
scaled

and chill
the slack
and dimple

of the rump.
Pout
the mouth,

brow the eyes
and now
and now

eclipse
in these hips,
these loins

the moon,
the blood
flux.

It's done.
I turn,
I flab upward

blub-lipped,
hipless
and I am

sexless,
shed
of ecstasy,

a pale
swimmer,
sequin-skinned,

pearling eggs
screamlessly
in seaweed.

It's what
I set my heart on.
Yet

ruddering
and muscling
in the sunless tons

of new freedoms,
still
I feel

a chill pull,
a brightening,
a light, a light,

and how
in my loomy cold,
my greens,

still
she moons
in me.

9

Night Feed

This is dawn.
Believe me
This is your season, little daughter.
The moment daisies open,
The hour mercurial rainwater
Makes a mirror for sparrows.
It's time we drowned our sorrows.

I tiptoe in.
I lift you up
Wriggling
In your rosy, zipped sleeper.
Yes, this is the hour
For the early bird and me
When finder is keeper.

I crook the bottle.
How you suckle!
This is the best I can be,
Housewife
To this nursery
Where you hold on,
Dear life.

A silt of milk.
The last suck.
And now your eyes are open,
Birth-coloured and offended.
Earth wakes.
You go back to sleep.
The feed is ended.

Worms turn.
Stars go in.
Even the moon is losing face.
Poplars stilt for dawn
And we begin
The long fall from grace.
I tuck you in.

The Oral Tradition

I was standing there
at the end of a reading
or a workshop or whatever,
watching people heading
out into the weather,

only half-wondering
what becomes of words,
the brisk herbs of language,
the fragrances we think we sing,
if anything.

We were left behind
in a firelit room
in which the colour scheme
crouched well down –
golds, a sort of dun

a distressed ochre –
and the sole richness was
in the suggestion of a texture
like the low flax gleam
that comes off polished leather.

Two women
were standing in shadow,
one with her back turned.
Their talk was a gesture,
an outstretched hand.

They talked to each other
and words like 'summer'
'birth' 'great-grandmother'
kept pleading with me,
urging me to follow.

'She could feel it coming' –
one of them was saying –
 'all the way there,
across the fields at evening
and no one there, God help her

'and she had on a skirt
of cross-woven linen
and the little one
kept pulling at it.
It was nearly night . . .'

(Wood hissed and split
in the open grate,
broke apart in sparks,
a windfall of light
in the room's darkness)

'. . . when she lay down
and gave birth to him
in an open meadow.
What a child that was
to be born without a blemish!'

It had started raining,
the windows dripping, misted.
One moment I was standing
not seeing out,
only half-listening

staring at the night; the next
without warning
I was caught by it:
the bruised summer light,
the musical sub-text

of mauve eaves on lilac
and the laburnum past
and shadow where the lime
tree dropped its bracts
in frills of contrast

where she lay down
in vetch and linen
and lifted up her son
to the archive
they would shelter in:

the oral song
avid as superstition,
layered like an amber in
the wreck of language
and the remnants of a nation.

I was getting out
my coat, buttoning it,
shrugging up the collar.
It was bitter outside,
a real winter's night

and I had distances
ahead of me: iron miles
in trains, iron rails
repeating instances
and reasons; the wheels

singing innuendoes, hints,
outlines underneath
the surface, a sense
suddenly of truth,
its resonance.

The Journey

for Elizabeth Ryle

Immediately cries were heard. These were the loud wailing of infant
souls weeping at the very entrance-way; never had they had their
share of life's sweetness for the dark day had stolen them from their
mothers' breasts and plunged them to a death before their time.
  Virgil, The Aeneid, Book VI

And then the dark fell and 'there has never'
I said 'been a poem to an antibiotic:
never a word to compare with the odes on
the flower of the raw sloe for fever

'or the devious Africa-seeking tern
or the protein treasures of the sea-bed.
Depend on it, somewhere a poet is wasting
his sweet uncluttered metres on the obvious

'emblem instead of the real thing.
Instead of sulpha we shall have hyssop dipped
in the wild blood of the unblemished lamb,
so every day the language gets less

'for the task and we are less with the language.'
I finished speaking and the anger faded
and dark fell and the book beside me
lay open at the page Aphrodite

comforts Sappho in her love's duress.
The poplars shifted their music in the garden,
a child startled in a dream,
my room was a mess –

the usual hardcovers, half-finished cups,
clothes piled up on an old chair –
and I was listening out but in my head was
a loosening and sweetening heaviness,

not sleep, but nearly sleep, not dreaming really
but as ready to believe and still
unfevered, calm and unsurprised
when she came and stood beside me

and I would have known her anywhere
and I would have gone with her anywhere
and she came wordlessly
and without a word I went with her

down down down without so much as
ever touching down but always, always
with a sense of much beneath us,
the way of stairs winding down to a river

and as we went on the light went on
failing and I looked sideways to be certain
it was she, misshapen, musical
Sappho – the scholiast's nightingale

and down we went, again down
until we came to a sudden rest
beside a river in what seemed to be
an oppressive suburb of the dawn.

My eyes got slowly used to the bad light.
At first I saw shadows, only shadows.
Then I could make out women and children
and, in the way they were, the grace of love.

'Cholera, typhus, croup, diptheria,'
she said, 'in those days they racketed
in every backstreet and alley of old Europe.
Behold the children of the plague.'

Then to my horror I could see to each
nipple some had clipped a limpet shape –
suckling darknesses – while others had their arms
weighed down, making terrible pietàs.

She took my sleeve and said to me, 'Be careful.
Do not define these women by their work:
not as washerwomen trussed in dust and sweating,
muscling water into linen by the river's edge

'nor as court ladies brailled in silk
on wool and woven with an ivory unicorn
and hung, nor as laundresses tossing cotton,
brisking daylight with lavender and gossip.

'But these are women who went out like you
when dusk became a dark sweet with leaves,
recovering the day, stooping, picking up
teddy bears and rag dolls and tricycles and buckets –

'love's archeology – and they too like you
stood boot deep in flowers once in summer
or saw winter come in with a single magpie
in a caul of haws, a solo harlequin.'

I stood fixed. I could not reach or speak to them.
Between us was the melancholy river,
the dream water, the narcotic crossing
and they had passed over it, its cold persuasions.

I whispered, 'Let me be
let me at least be their witness,' but she said
'What you have seen is beyond speech,
beyond song, only not beyond love;

remember it, you will remember it'
and I heard her say but she was fading fast
as we emerged under the stars of heaven,
'there are not many of us; you are dear

'and stand beside me as my own daughter.
I have brought you here so you will know forever
the silences in which are our beginnings,
in which we have an origin like water,'

and the wind shifted and the window clasp
opened, banged and I woke up to find
MY the poetry books stacked higgledy-piggledy,
my skirt spread out where I had laid it –

nothing was changed; nothing was more clear
but it was wet and the year was late.
The rain was grief in arrears; my children
slept the last dark out safely and I wept.

Fond Memory

It was a school where all the children wore darned worsted;
where they cried – or almost all – when the Reverend Mother
announced at lunch-time that the King had died

peacefully in his sleep. I dressed in wool as well,
ate rationed food, played English games and learned
how wise the Magna Carta was, how hard the Hanoverians

had tried, the measure and complexity of verse,
the hum and score of the whole orchestra.
At three o'clock I caught two buses home

where sometimes in the late afternoon
at a piano pushed into a corner of the playroom
my father would sit down and play the slow

lilts of Tom Moore while I stood there trying
not to weep at the cigarette smoke stinging up
from between his fingers and – as much as I could think –

I thought this is my country, was, will be again,
this upward-straining song made to be
our safe inventory of pain. And I was wrong.

The Black Lace Fan My Mother Gave Me

It was the first gift he ever gave her,
buying it for five francs in the Galeries
in pre-war Paris. It was stifling.
A starless drought made the nights stormy.

They stayed in the city for the summer.
They met in cafés. She was always early.
He was late. That evening he was later.
They wrapped the fan. He looked at his watch.

She looked down the Boulevard des Capucines.
She ordered more coffee. She stood up.
The streets were emptying. The heat was killing.
She thought the distance smelled of rain and lightning.

These are wild roses, appliqued on silk by hand,
darkly picked, stitched boldly, quickly.
The rest is tortoiseshell and has the reticent,
clear patience of its element. It is

a worn-out underwater bullion and it keeps,
even now, an inference of its violation.
The lace is overcast as if the weather
it opened for and offset had entered it.

The past is an empty café terrace.
An airless dusk before thunder. A man running.
And no way now to know what happened then –
none at all – unless, of course, you improvise:

The blackbird on this first sultry morning,
in summer, finding buds, worms, fruit,
feels the heat. Suddenly she puts out her wing –
the whole, full, flirtatious span of it.

We Were Neutral in the War

This warm, late summer there is so much
to get in. The ladder waits by the crab apple tree.
The greenhouse is rank with the best
Irish tomatoes. Pears are ripening.

Your husband frowns at dinner, has no time
for the baby who has learned to crease three
fingers and wave 'day-day.' This is serious,
he says. This could be what we all feared.

You pierce a sequin with a needle.
You slide it down single-knotted thread
until it ties with all the others in
a puzzle of brightness. Then another and another one.

Let the green and amber marrows rise up
and beat against it and the crab apples and
the damson-coloured pram by the back
wall: you will not sew them into it.

The wooden ledge of the conservatory
faces south. Row on row,
the pears are laid out there, are hard
and then yellow and then yellow with

a rosiness. You leave them out of it.
They will grow soft and bruised at the top
and rot, all in one afternoon. The light,
which made them startling, you will use.

On the breakfast table the headlines are
telling of a city under threat where
you mixed cheese with bitter fennel
and fell in love over demitasse. Afterwards,

you walked by the moonlit river and stopped
and looked down. A glamorous circumference is
spinning on your needle, is
that moon in satin water making

the same peremptory demands on
the waves of the Irish sea and as each
salt-window opens to reveal
a weather of agates, you will stitch that in

with the orchard colours of the first preserves
you make from the garden. You move the jars from
the pantry to the windowsill where
you can see them: winter jewels.

The night he comes to tell you this is war
you wait for him to put on his dinner jacket.
The party is tonight.
The streets are quiet. Dublin is at peace.

The talk is of death but you take
the hand of the first man who asks you.
You dance the fox-trot, the two-step,
the quickstep,

in time to the music. Exclusions
glitter at your hips and past and future are
the fended-off and far-fetched
in waltz time below your waist.

The Achill Woman

She came up the hill carrying water.
She wore half-buttoned, wool cardigan,
a tea-towel round her waist.

She pushed the hair out of her eyes with
her free hand and put the bucket down.

The zinc-music of the handle on the rim
tuned the evening. An Easter moon rose.
In the next-door field a stream was
a fluid sunset; and then, stars.

I remember the cold rosiness of her hands.
She bent down and blew on them like broth.
And round her waist, on a white background,
in coarse, woven letters, the words 'glass cloth.'

And she was nearly finished for the day.
And I was all talk, raw from college –
weekending at a friend's cottage
with one suitcase and the set text
of the Court poets of the Silver Age.

We stayed putting down time until
the evening turned cold without warning.
She said goodnight and started down the hill.

The grass changed from lavender to black.
The trees turned back to cold outlines.
You could taste frost

but nothing now can change the way I went
indoors, chilled by the wind
and made a fire
and took down my book
and opened it and failed to comprehend

the harmonies of servitude,
the grace music gives to flattery
and language borrows from ambition –

and how I fell asleep
oblivious to

the planets clouding over in the skies,
the slow decline of the Spring moon,
the songs crying out their ironies.

What We Lost

It is a winter afternoon.
The hills are frozen. Light is failing.
The distance is a crystal earshot.
A woman is mending linen in her kitchen.

She is a countrywoman.
Behind her cupboard doors she hangs sprigged,
stove-dried lavender in muslin.
Her letters and mementoes and memories

are packeted in satin at the back with
gaberdine and worsted and
the cambric she has made into bodices;
the good tobacco silk for Sunday Mass.

She is sewing in the kitchen.
The sugar-feel of flax is in her hands.
Dusk. And the candles brought in then.
One by one. And the quiet sweat of wax.

There is a child at her side.
The tea is poured, the stitching put down.
The child grows still, sensing something of importance.
The woman settles and begins her story.

Believe it, what we lost is here in this room
on this veiled evening.
The woman finishes. The story ends.
The child, who is my mother, gets up, moves away.

In the winter air, unheard, unshared,
the moment happens, hangs fire, leads nowhere.
The light will fail and the room darken,
the child fall asleep and the story be forgotten.

The fields are dark already.
The frail connections have been made and are broken.
The dumb-show of legend has become language,
is becoming silence and who will know that once

words were possibilities and disappointments,
were scented closets filled with love letters
and memories and lavender hemmed into muslin,
stored in sachets, aired in bed linen;

and traveled silks and the tones of cotton
tautened into bodices, subtly shaped by breathing;
were the rooms of childhood with their griefless peace,
their hands and whispers, their candles weeping brightly?

That the Science of Cartography Is Limited

– and not simply by the fact that this shading of
forest cannot show the fragrance of balsam,
the gloom of cypresses
is what I wish to prove.

When you and I were first in love we drove
to the borders of Connacht
and entered a wood there.

Look down you said: this was once a famine road.

I looked down at ivy and the scutch grass
rough-cast stone had
disappeared into as you told me
in the second winter of their ordeal, in

1847, when the crop had failed twice,
Relief Committees gave
the starving Irish such roads to build.

Where they died, there the road ended

and ends still and when I take down
the map of this island, it is never so
I can say here is
the masterful, the apt rendering of

the spherical as flat, nor
an ingenious design which persuades a curve
into a plane,
but to tell myself again that

the line which says woodland and cries hunger
and gives out among sweet pine and cypress,
and finds no horizon

will not be there.

The Dolls Museum in Dublin

The wounds are terrible. The paint is old.
The cracks along the lips and on the cheeks
cannot be fixed. The cotton lawn is soiled.
The arms are ivory dissolved to wax.

Recall the Quadrille. Hum the waltz.
Promenade on the yachtclub terraces.
Put back the lamps in their copper holders.
The carriage wheels on the cobbled quays.

And re-create Easter in Dublin.
Booted officers. Their mistresses.
Sunlight criss-crossing College Green.
Steam hissing from the flanks of horses.

Here they are. Cradled and cleaned.
Held close in the arms of their owners.
Their cold hands clasped by warm hands,
Their faces memorized like perfect manners.

The altars are mannerly with linen.
The lilies are whiter than surplices.
The candles are burning and warning:
Rejoice, they whisper. After sacrifice.

Horse chestnuts hold up their candles.
The Green is vivid with parasols.
Sunlight is pastel and windless.
The bar of the Shelbourne is full.

Laughter and gossip on the terraces.
Rumour and alarm at the barracks.
The Empire is summoning its officers.
The carriages are turning: they are turning back.

Past children walking with governesses,
looking down, cossetting their dolls,
then looking up as the carriage passes,
the shadow chilling them. Twilight falls.

It is twilight in the dolls' museum. Shadows
remain on the parchment-coloured waists,
are bruises on the stitched cotton clothes,
are hidden in the dimples on the wrists.

The eyes are wide. They cannot address
the helplessness which has lingered in,
the airless peace of each glass case:
To have survived. To have been stronger than

a moment. To be the hostages ignorance
takes from time and ornament from destiny. Both.
To be the present of the past. To infer the difference
with a terrible stare. But not feel it. And not know it.

The Pomegranate

The only legend I have ever loved is
The story of a daughter lost in hell.
And found and rescued there.
Love and blackmail are the gist of it.
Ceres and Persephone the names.
And the best thing about the legend is
I can enter it anywhere. And have.
As a child in exile in
A city of fogs and strange consonants,
I read it first and at first I was
An exiled child in the crackling dusk of
The underworld, the stars blighted. Later
I walked out in a summer twilight
Searching for my daughter at bed-time.
When she came running I was ready
To make any bargain to keep her.
I carried her back past whitebeams
And wasps and honey-scented buddleias.
But I was Ceres then and I knew
Winter was in store for every leaf
On every tree on that road.
Was inescapable for each one we passed.
And for me.
It is winter
And the stars are hidden.
I climb the stairs and stand where I can see
My child asleep beside her teen magazines,
Her can of Coke, her plate of uncut fruit.
The pomegranate! How did I forget it?
She could have come home and been safe
And ended the story and all
Our heart-broken searching but she reached
Out a hand and plucked a pomegranate.
She put out her hand and pulled down
The French sound for apple and
The noise of stone and the proof
That even in the place of death,

At the heart of legend, in the midst
Of rocks full of unshed tears
Ready to be diamonds by the time
The story was told, a child can be
Hungry. I could warn her. There is still a chance.
The rain is cold. The road is flint-coloured.
The suburb has cars and cable television.
The veiled stars are above ground.
It is another world. But what else
Can a mother give her daughter but such
Beautiful rifts in time?
If I defer the grief I will diminish the gift.
The legend will be hers as well as mine.
She will enter it. Must As I have.
She will wake up. She will hold
The papery, flushed skin in her hand.
And to her lips. I will say nothing.

At the Glass Factory in Cavan Town

Today it is a swan:
        The guide tells us
these are in demand.
        The glass is made

of red lead and potash
        and the smashed bits
of crystal sinews
        and decanter stoppers

crated over there –
        she points – and shattered
on the stone wheel
        rimmed with emery.

Aromas of stone and
        fire. Deranged singing
from the grindstone.
        And behind that

a mirror – my
        daughters' heads turned
away in it – garnering
        grindstone and fire.

The glass blower goes
        to the furnace.
He takes a pole
        from the earth's

core: the earth's core
        is remembered in
the molten globe at
        the end of it.

He shakes the pole
          carefully to and fro.
He blows once. Twice.
          His cheeks puff and

puff up: he is
          a cherub at the very
edge of a cornice with
          a mouthful of zephyrs –

sweet intrusions into
          leaves and lace hems.
And now he lays
          the rod on its spindle.

It is red. It is
          ruddy and cooler.
It is cool now
          and as clear as

the distances of this
          county with its drumlins,
its herons, its closed-
          in waterways on which

we saw this morning
          as we drove over
here, a mated pair
          of swans. Such

blind grace as they
          floated with told us
they did not know
          that every hour,

every day, and
          not far away from
there, they were
          entering the legend of

themselves. They gave no
        sign of it. But what
caught my eye, my
        attention, was the safety

they assumed as
        they sailed their own
images. Here, now –
        and knowing that

the mirror still holds
        my actual flesh –
I could say to them:
        reflection is the first

myth of loss, but
        they floated away and
away from me as if
        no one would ever blow

false airs on them
        or try their sinews
in the fire, at
        the core, and they

took no care
        not to splinter, they
showed no fear
        they would end as

this one which is
        uncut yet still might:
a substance of its own
        future form, both

fraction and refraction
        in the deal-wood
crate at the door
        we will leave by.

Anna Liffey

Life, the story goes,
Was the daughter of Cannan,
And came to the plain of Kildare.
She loved the flatlands and the ditches
And the unreachable horizon.
She asked that it be named for her.
The river took its name from the land.
The land took its name from a woman.

*

A woman in the doorway of a house.
A river in the city of her birth.

*

There, in the hills above my house,
The river Liffey rises, is a source.
It rises in rush and ling heather and
Black peat and bracken and strengthens
To claim the city it narrated.
Swans. Steep falls. Small towns.
The smudged air and bridges of Dublin.

*

Dusk is coming.
Rain is moving east from the hills.

*

If I could see myself
I would see
A woman in a doorway
Wearing the colours that go with red hair.
Although my hair is no longer red.

*

I praise
The gifts of the river.
Its shiftless and glittering

31

Retelling of a city,
Its clarity as it flows,
In the company of runt flowers and herons,
Around a bend at Islandbridge
And under thirteen bridges to the sea.
Its patience at twilight –
Swans nesting by it,
Neon wincing into it.

*

Maker of
Places, remembrances,
Narrate such fragments for me:

One body. One spirit.
One place. One name.
The city where I was born.
The river that runs through it.
The nation which eludes me.

Fractions of a life
It has taken me a lifetime
To claim.

*

I came here in a cold winter.

I had no children. No country.
I did not know the name for my own life.

My country took hold of me.
My children were born.

I walked out in a summer dusk
To call them in.

One name. Then the other one.
The beautiful vowels sounding out home.

*

Make a nation what you will
Make of the past
What you can –

There is now
A woman in a doorway.

It has taken me
All my strength to do this.

Becoming a figure in a poem.

Usurping a name and a theme.

*

A river is not a woman.
    Although the names it finds,
        The history it makes
And suffers –
    The Viking blades beside it,
        The muskets of the Redcoats,
            The flames of the Four Courts
Blazing into it –
    Are a sign.
        Any more than
A woman is a river,
    Although the course it takes,
        Through swans courting and distraught willows,
Its patience
    Which is also its powerlessness,
        From Callary to Islandbridge,
            And from source to mouth,
Is another one.
                And in my late forties
Past believing
  Love will heal
    What language fails to know
And needs to say –
    What the body means –

I take this sign
And I make this mark:
    A woman in the doorway of her house.
    A river in the city of her birth.
The truth of a suffered life.
    The mouth of it.

    *

The seabirds come in from the coast.
The city wisdom is they bring rain.
I watch them from my doorway.
I see them as arguments of origin –
Leaving a harsh force on the horizon,
Only to find it
Slanting and falling elsewhere.

Which water –
The one they leave or the one they pronounce –
Remembers the other?

I am sure
The body of an ageing woman
Is a memory
And to find a language for it
Is as hard
As weeping and requiring
These birds to cry out as if they could
Recognize their element
Remembered and diminished in
A single tear.

    *

An ageing woman
Finds no shelter in language.
She finds instead
Single words she once loved
Such as 'summer' and 'yellow'
And 'sexual' and 'ready'
Have suddenly become dwellings

34

For someone else –
Rooms and a roof under which someone else
Is welcome, not her. Tell me,
Anna Liffey,
Spirit of water,
Spirit of place,
How is it on this
Rainy Autumn night
As the Irish sea takes
The names you made, the names
You bestowed, and gives you back
Only wordlessness?

*

Autumn rain is
Scattering and dripping
From car-ports
And clipped hedges.
The gutters are full.

When I came here
I had neither
Children nor country.
The trees were arms.
The hills were dreams.

I was free
To imagine a spirit
In the blues and greens,
The hills and fogs
Of a small city.

My children were born.
My country took hold of me.
A vision in a brick house.
Is it only love
That makes a place?

I feel it change.
My children are
Growing up, getting older.
My country holds on
To its own pain.

I turn off
The harsh yellow
Porch light and
Stand in the hall.
Where is home now?

Follow the rain
Out to the Dublin hills.
Let it become the river.
Let the spirit of place be
A lost soul again.

          *

In the end
It will not matter
That I was a woman. I am sure of it.
The body is a source. Nothing more.
There is a time for it. There is a certainty
About the way it seeks its own dissolution.
Consider rivers.
They are always en route to
Their own nothingness. From the first moment
They are going home. And so
When language cannot do it for us,
Cannot make us know love will not diminish us,
There are these phrases
Of the ocean
To console us.
Particular and unafraid of their completion.
In the end
Everything that burdened and distinguished me
Will be lost in this:
I was a voice.

A Woman Painted on a Leaf

I found it among curios and silver,
in the pureness of wintry light.

A woman painted on a leaf.

Fine lines drawn on a veined surface
in a hand-made frame.

This is not my face. Neither did I draw it.

A leaf falls in a garden.
The moon cools its aftermath of sap.
The pith of summer dries out in starlight.

A woman is inscribed there.

This is not death. It is the terrible
suspension of life.

I want a poem
I can grow old in. I want a poem I can die in.

I want to take
this dried-out face,
as you take a starling from behind iron,
and return it to its element of air, of ending –

so that Autumn
which was once
the hard look of stars,
the frown on a gardener's face,
a gradual bronzing of the distance,

will be,
from now on,
a crisp tinder underfoot. Cheekbones. Eyes. Will be
a mouth crying out. Let me.

Let me die.

The Harbour

This harbour was made by art and force.
And called Kingstown and afterwards Dun Laoghaire.
And holds the sea behind its barrier
less than five miles from my house.

Lord be with us say the makers of a nation.
Lord look down say the builders of a harbour.
They came and cut a shape out of ocean
and left stone to close around their labour.

Officers and their wives promenaded
on this spot once and saw with their own eyes
the opulent horizon and obedient skies
which nine tenths of the law provided.

And frigates with thirty-six guns, cruising
the outer edges of influence, could idle
and enter here and catch the tide of
empire and arrogance and the Irish Sea rising

and rising through a century of storms
and cormorants and moonlight the whole length of this coast,
while an ocean forgot an empire and the armed
ships under it changed: to slime weed and cold salt and rust.

City of shadows and of the gradual
capitulations to the last invader
this is the final one: signed in water
and witnessed in granite and ugly bronze and gun-metal.

And by me. I am your citizen: composed of
your fictions, your compromise, I am
a part of your story and its outcome.
And ready to record its contradictions.

Home

for Jody Allen-Randolph

Off a side road in southern California
is a grove of eucalyptus.
It looks as if
someone once came here with a handful

of shadows not seeds and planted them.
And they turned into trees.
But the leaves
have a tell-tale blueness and deepness.

Up a slope to the left is a creek.
Across it lies a cut-down tree trunk.
Further back again is the faraway,
filtered-out glitter of the Pacific.

I went there one morning with a friend
in mid-October
when the monarch butterflies
arrive from their westward migration:

thousands of them. Hundreds of thousands
collecting in a single location.

I climbed to the creek and looked up.
Every leaf was covered and ended in
a fluttering struggle.

Atmosphere. Ocean. Oxygen and dust
were altered by their purposes:
They had changed the trees to iron.
They were rust.

I looked at my watch. It was early.
But my mind was ready
for the evening
they were darkening into overhead:

Every inch and atom of daylight
was filled with their beating and flitting,
their rising and flying at the hour
when dusk falls on a coastal city

where I had my hands full of shadows.
Once. And planted them.
And they became
a suburb and a house and a doorway
entered by and open to an evening
every room was lighted to offset.

I once thought that a single word
had the power to change.
To transform.

But these had not been changed.
And I would not be changed by it again.

If I could not say the word *home*.
If I could not breathe the Irish night
air and influence of rain coming from the east,

I could at least be sure –
far below them and unmoved by movement –
of one house with its window, making

an oblong of wheat out of light.

Dublin, 1959

The café had
plastic chairs and lunch counters.
Its doors opened out on O'Connell Street.

I hunched my knees
under the table. The vinegar bottle
shifted its bitter yellows.

Tell me a story about Ireland
I said as a child
to anyone in earshot: about what had been
left behind by a modern world.
But not by memory.

I remember
we paid for our tea with a single pound note.
And walked out. And a bicycle went by,
its bell ringing loudly. And a car swerved around it.

The Last Discipline

In the evening
after a whole day at the easel
my mother would put down her brush,
pour turpentine into a glass jar,
and walk to the table.

Then she took a mirror,
hand-sized, enamelled in green,
and turned her back to the canvas.
And stood there.
And looked in it.

It was dusk.
The sheets were ghostly.
The canvas was almost not there.
In the end all I could see was her hand
closed around the handle.

All I can see now
is her hand, her head.
Her back is turned to what she made.
The mirror shows her
what is over her shoulder:

a room in winter.
A window with fog outside it.
A painting she sees is not finished.
A child. Her face round with impatience,
who will return,

who has returned,
who only knows now that she has seen
the rare and necessary –
usually unobservable –
last discipline.

The Necessity for Irony

On Sundays,
when the rain held off,
after lunch or later,
I would go with my twelve year old
daughter into town,
and put down the time
at junk sales, antique fairs.

There I would
lean over tables,
absorbed by
lace, wooden frames,
glass. My daughter stood
at the other end of the room,
her flame-coloured hair
obvious whenever –
which was not often –

I turned around.
I turned around.
She was gone.
Grown. No longer ready
to come with me, whenever
a dry Sunday
held out its promises
of small histories. Endings.

When I was young
I studied styles: their use
and origin. Which age
was known for which
ornament: and was always drawn
to a lyric speech, a civil tone.
But never thought
I would have the need,
as I do now, for a darker one:

Spirit of irony,
my caustic author
of the past, of memory, –
and of its pain, which returns
hurts, stings – reproach me now,
remind me
that I was in those rooms,
with my child,
with my back turned to her,
searching – oh irony! –
for beautiful things.

Eiléan Ní Chuilleanáin

The Lady's Tower

Hollow my high tower leans
Back to the cliff; my thatch
Converses with spread sky,
Heronries. The grey wall
Slices downward and meets
A sliding flooded stream
Pebble-banked, small diving
Birds. Downstairs my cellars plumb.

Behind me shifting the oblique veins
Of the hill; my kitchen is damp,
Spiders shaded under brown vats.

I hear the stream change pace, glance from the stove
To see the punt is now floating freely
Bobs square-ended, the rope dead-level.

Opening the kitchen door
The quarry brambles miss my hair
Sprung so high their fruit wastes.

And up the tall stairs my bed is made
Even with a sycamore root
At my small square window.

All night I lie sheeted, my broom chases down treads
Delighted spirals of dust: the yellow duster glides
Over shelves, around knobs: bristle stroking flagstone
Dancing with the spiders around the kitchen in the dark
While cats climb the tower and the river fills
A spoonful of light on the cellar walls below.

Lucina Schynning in Silence of the Nicht

Moon shining in silence of the night
The heaven being all full of stars
I was reading my book in a ruin
By a sour candle, without roast meat or music
Strong drink of a shield from the air
Blowing in the crazed window, and I felt
Moonlight on my head, clear after three days' rain.

I washed in cold water; it was orange, channelled down bogs
Dipped between cresses.
The bats flew through my room where I slept safely.
Sheep stared at me when I woke.

Behind me the waves of darkness lay, the plague
Of mice, plague of beetles
Crawling out of the spines of books,
Plague shadowing pale faces with clay
The disease of the moon gone astray.

In the desert I relaxed, amazed
As the mosaic beasts on the chapel floor
When Cromwell had departed, and they saw
The sky growing through the hole in the roof.

Sheepdogs embraced me; the grasshopper
Returned with lark and bee.
I looked down between hedges of high thorn and saw
The hare, absorbed, sitting still
In the middle of the track; I heard
Again the chirp of the stream running.

Now

I am walking beside Sandymount strand,
Not on it; the tide is nearly at the new wall.
Four children are pushing back and forth
A huge reel that has held electric cable
They are knee deep in the water
I come closer and see they have rubber boots on.

The sand looks level but the water lies here and there
Searching out valleys an inch deep. They interlock
Reflecting a bright morning sky.
A man with a hat says to me 'Is it coming in or going out?'
He is not trying to start something, the weather is too fine
The hour early. 'Coming in I think' I say
I have been watching one patch getting smaller.

Other people are taking large dogs for walks.
Have they no work to go to? The old baths
Loom square like a mirage.
Light glances off water, wet sand and houses;
Just now I am passing Maurice Craig's
And there he is reading a book at his window.
It is a quarter past ten –
He looks as if he's been at it for hours.

Swineherd

When all this is over, said the swineherd,
I mean to retire, where
Nobody will have heard about my special skills
And conversation is mainly about the weather.

I intend to learn how to make coffee, at least as well
As the Portuguese lay-sister in the kitchen
And polish the brass fenders every day.
I want to lie awake at night
Listening to cream crawling to the top of the jug
And the water lying soft in the cistern.

I want to see an orchard where the trees grow in straight lines
And the yellow fox finds shelter between the navy-blue trunks,
Where it gets dark early in summer
And the apple-blossom is allowed to wither on the bough.

The Second Voyage

Odysseus rested on his oar and saw
The ruffled foreheads of the waves
Crocodiling and mincing past: he rammed
The oar between their jaws and looked down
In the simmering sea where scribbles of weed defined
Uncertain depth, and the slim fishes progressed
In fatal formation, and thought

                            If there was a single
Streak of decency in these waves now, they'd be ridged
Pocked and dented with the battering they've had,
And we could name them as Adam named the beasts,
Saluting a new one with dismay, or a notorious one
With admiration; they'd notice us passing
And rejoice at our shipwreck, but these
Have less character than sheep and need more patience.

I know what I'll do he said;
I'll park my ship in the crook of a long pier
(And I'll take you with me he said to the oar)
I'll face the rising ground and walk away
From tidal waters, up riverbeds
Where herons parcel out the miles of stream,
Over gaps in the hills, through warm
Silent valleys, and when I meet a farmer
Bold enough to look me in the eye
With 'where are you off to with that long
Winnowing fan over your shoulder?'
There I will stand still
And I'll plant you for a gatepost or a hitching-post
And leave you as a tidemark. I can go back
And organise my house then.

But the profound
Unfenced valleys of the ocean still held him;
He had only the oar to make them keep their distance;
The sea was still frying under the ship's side.
He considered the water-lilies, and thought about fountains
Spraying as wide as willows in empty squares,
The sugarstick of water clattering into the kettle,
The flat lakes bisecting the rushes. He remembered spiders
      and frogs
Housekeeping at the roadside in brown trickles floored
      with mud,
Horsetroughs, the black canal, pale swans at dark:
His face grew damp with tears that tasted
Like his own sweat or the insults of the sea.

Survivors

Where the loose wheel swings at the stern
Of Noah's ark, I can see the man himself
Deathmask profile against a late sunrise
Bleeding profusely from a wound in his throat.

On deck the mouse wakes up, stretches,
Edges to shelter to watch the cat.
The other mouse has stopped trying to distract him.
She does not know the beasts of prey
Have all been brainwashed. Their ascetic pose
Should last the voyage.

No winds compel us eastward or
Westward propel seeds of plants
Or the smell of decomposing systems.
If the water drains we may see
Again our flooded springtime, scarred
With damp, leaves clinging together
Like the pages of a sunk book,
The graves of the dead washed clean.

The bloodstained shirt stiffens
Turns brown at the shoulder; the blood
Edges down the sleeve, soft with a fresh smell.

The animals think they are being taken somewhere.
Do they all want to survive? They allow me
To lock their kennels at sunset, feed them
Turnips, even the carnivores.
Their drink is juice of the flood.

Please go easy with the blood.
It's not as if we had that much to spare;
The human ration has been cut
To a gallon a head, and the heads have been cut
As a temporary measure to me and you.

The menagerie expects a future and you
Crouching on the deck against my knees
Let it drip on my wet skirt
Soak in with dust and rain
Lodged firmly until the blood of the saints
Rises vertically smelling of ink
From sawdust, flagstones, seacaves, to explain.
While the blood still seeps down
I drink it steadily myself
(I have to think of the passengers)
My teeth ploughing in your throat.

I feel now so old I can barely remember
How it was before I was conceived.
I recall a shining egg-shaped ocean
Foul as a deserted egg;
It weighed down on the sea bed
Like the fat arse of Leviathan
Pressing the lives out of lobsters, cracking the ribs of wrecks;
Nothing was able to move.
How peaceful it was, long ago!

Acts and Monuments

In imitation of the weed
Which, out of soft enclosing mud
As from a hand that holds a lead
Leans after the escaping flood,

Or when warm summer stunts the flow
In tangled coils lies tired and fine,
Or in calm weather stands tiptoe
To peer above the waterline,

The rooted trees bend in the wind
Or twist and bow on every side;
The poplar stands up straight and slim;
But their blood cannot flower or fade

Like weeds that rot when rivers dry.
Their roots embrace the stony plain,
Their branches move as one, they try
To freeze the effects of wind and rain.

And like the waterline the sky
Lids and defines the element
Where no unformed capricious cry
Can sound without its monument.

A Midwinter Prayer

In winter's early days, the exile takes the road –
Dangerous nights with ghosts abroad:
The eve of Samhain in the High King's hall
Fionn stood all night, his eyes open
For well-armed demons, for fire, music and death.

The wanderer catches light from chapel doors.

(He recalls a little boy running
Up and down the same steps
Doing the Ins and Outs:
A Plenary Indulgence every five minutes
To lighten the penance of Fenian men
Awaiting liberation from demons underground.)

In silence the festival begins,
Human words are all spilled and soaked into the brown earth.
The silent holiday of Munster
Where the dead lie more at ease
Warmer than ever under the loud northern
Remembrance. The uprooted love
That fed them once collapses
Into their graves like cut flowers.

The final Sunday after Pentecost the priest
Announced the Last Day, when the dead will spring
Like shrubs from quaking earth.
Against that spring the dark night sways
Swelling grey plumes of smoke over the edge of the world.

(He sees, westward again, the islands
Floating lightly as bunches of foam
Alongside the neat schooner. There
Yellow apples constantly in season
Bend high branches, and the exile
Is comforted in an orchard.)

The road stretches like the soul's posthumous journey.
The holly-trees were falling already
When he left; the delicate high houses were rotting
In rain.

(He could remember summer barricades
Defended on top by a row of nettles)

And all his life seemed like a funeral journey
And all his company a troop
Of anxious gravediggers.

– And is that the young son
I carried through the wet and dry months?
Said the mother.

The air turned cold
Icicles began to grow,
Frost enamelled windows
And branches bent under snow.
All that the cold touched, alive or dead,
Changed. A time of plenty:
Ships tied up at the quay
Unloading crates of raisins, mandarins.
Yellow apples for the feast.

Touched by cold, the girl gave birth in a ruin:
Frost made angels echo behind the sky;
The cold stars offered gifts of incense and hard gold.
The snow spared the growing seed
As the year swung round to a new birth.

The exile is a wise man with a star and stable;
He is an unpeopled poet staring at a broken wall.
He tours the excavations of east and west,
He sleeps in a cart by a river
Blocked by old barbed wire and dead dogs.

When February stirs the weeds
He'll start again moving to the west
Rounding the earth to recover his lost islands.
He shelters in the ruined house
Where in dead silence the plaster falls
From ceilings, hour by hour. Those islands –
Under his skull, under wave, underground?

He walks the streets as the celebrations begin.
Work accelerates: turkeys are crated,
Bottles shift on shelves. He is jostled by baskets.

Now trampling feet remind his ears of hammers
Of a hundred smiths constructing the new model of the world

Turning in time to music or the circulation of the blood
Where love will not be out of season or a man out of place.
The seed laid in the dead earth of December
May yet grow to a flowering tree above ground.
He will sail in a ring of welcoming islands –
Midwinter, he can only pray to live that long.

Going Back to Oxford

Something to lose; it came in the equipment
Alongside the suicide pill and the dark blue card:
'I am a Catholic, please send for a priest'
With a space below for the next of kin.

Something to lose; and going back to Oxford,
Though not for good this time, I lose it again
As the city advances like an old relation
It's no use insulting.
Notice how she repeats her effects,
The Victorian towers after the mediaeval slum,
As a yawn turns into a shiver and the air
Bites like a mould pulling me north
To the evacuated roads.
Here the eye shrinks from what it sees,
The toothmarks are showing where the sharp spires got me;
And I agree to being chewed because
All that time I was looking for a reliable experience
And here it is: I give in every time,
Repeat the original despair.
This is where I learned it.

Because pleasure is astonishing, but loss
Expected, never at a loss for words;
Tearducts built in at birth: something to lose:
The best kind of innocence, which is not to have been afraid,
Lost according to plan; and here I am, walking
Through old streets to a familiar bed.

Early Recollections

If I produce paralysis in verse
Where anger would be more suitable,
Could it be because my education
Left out the sight of death?
They never waked my aunt Nora in the front parlour;
Our cats hunted mice but never
Showed us what they killed.
I was born in the war but never noticed.
My aunt Nora is still in the best of health
And her best china has not been changed or broken.
Dust has not settled on it; I noticed it first
The same year that I saw
How the colours of stones change as water
Dries off them after rain.
I know how things begin to happen
But never expect an end.

Dearest,
          if I can never write 'goodbye'
On the torn final sheet, do not
Investigate my adult life but try
Where I started. My
Childhood gave me hope
And no warnings.
I discovered the habits of moss
That secretly freezes the stone,
Rust softly biting the hinges
To keep the door always open.
I became aware of truth
Like the tide helplessly rising and falling in one place.

Wash

Wash man out of the earth; shear off
The human shell.
Twenty feet down there's close cold earth
So clean.

Wash the man out of the woman:
The strange sweat from her skin, the ashes from her hair.
Stretch her to dry in the sun
The blue marks on her breast will fade.

Woman and world not yet
Clean as the cat
Leaping to the windowsill with a fish in her teeth;
Her flat curious eyes reflect the squalid room,
She begins to wash the water from the fish.

Pygmalion's Image

Not only her stone face, laid back staring in the ferns,
But everything the scoop of the valley contains begins to move
(And beyond the horizon the trucks beat the highway.)

A tree inflates gently on the curve of the hill;
An insect crashes on the carved eyelid;
Grass blows westward from the roots,
As the wind knifes under her skin and ruffles it like a book.

The crisp hair is real, wriggling like snakes;
A rustle of veins, tick of blood in the throat;
The lines of the face tangle and catch, and
A green leaf of language comes twisting out of her mouth.

The Pig-boy

It was his bag of tricks she wanted, surely not him:
The pipkin that sat on the flame, its emissions
Transporting her so she skipped from kitchen to kitchen
Sampling licks of food; she knew who had bacon
And who had porridge and tea. And she needed
The swoop of light from his torch
That wavered as she walked,
Booted, through the evening fair,
Catching the green flash of sheep's eyes,
The glow of false teeth in the skull:

Its grotto light stroked oxters of arches,
Bridges, lintels, probed cobbles of tunnels
Where the world shook itself inside out like a knitted sleeve:
Light on the frozen mesh, the fishbone curve, the threads
And weights.
           And as day
Glittered on the skin, she stood
In the hood of a nostril and saw
The ocean gleam of his eye.

Street

He fell in love with the butcher's daughter
When he saw her passing by in her white trousers
Dangling a knife on a ring at her belt.
He stared at the dark shining drops on the paving-stones.

One day he followed her
Down the slanting lane at the back of the shambles.
A door stood half-open
And the stairs were brushed and clean,
Her shoes paired on the bottom step,
Each tread marked with the red crescent
Her bare heels left, fading to faintest at the top.

The Hill-town

The bus floats away on the big road and leaves her
In sunlight, the only moving thing to be seen.

The girl at her kitchen-window in the ramparts
Can glimpse her through a steep rift between houses.
She turns to salt the boiling water
As her mother begins to climb, dark blue in the blue shade,
Past the shut doors and the open windows,
Their sounds of knife and glass.
She crosses into the sun before passing
The blank shutters of the glazier's house.

He is in there, has heard her step and
Paused, with the sharp tool in his hand.
He stands, his fingers pressed against the looking-glass
Like a man trying to hold up a falling building
That is not even a reflection now.

Their child knows where to glance, turning off the flame,
To spot her mother, a wrinkle in the light.
She remembers lying in the wide bed, three years old,
The sound of water and the gas going silent,
And the morning was in the white sieve of the curtain
Where a shadow moved, her mother's body, wet patches
Blotting the stretched cloth, shining like dawn.

London

At fifty, she misses the breast
That grew in her thirteenth year
And was removed last month. She misses
The small car she drove through the seaside town
And along cliffs for miles. In London
She will not take the tube, is afraid of taxis.

We choose a random bar. She sits by me,
Looking along the jacketed line of men's

Lunchtime backs, drinks her vermouth.
I see her eye slide to the left;
At the counter's end sits a high metal urn.

What are you staring at? That polished curve,
The glint wavering on steel, the features
Of our stranger neighbour distorted.
You can't see it from where you are.
When that streak of crooked light
Goes out, my life is over.

River, with Boats

Of course she does not mind sleeping
On the deep fur of the bed
Beside the wide window
Where the birds hop,
Where the boats pass.

She can hear the hooters
Down there in a greeting;
She can see a flash of the river,
A glitter on the ceiling
When the wind blows
And the high branches of trees
On the other bank
Skip and bow in circles.

Only at the highest tide
The window is blocked
By the one framed eye
Of a tethered coaster
Swaying and tugging and flapping with the wind,
And the faces of the mariners
Crowd at the glass like fishes.

The Italian Kitchen

Time goes by the book laid open
On the long marble table: my work
In the kitchen your landlord painted yellow and white.
Beyond it the glass cupboard doors: behind them now
Ranged the green and yellow cups and plates
You bought in September and left behind, still in boxes.

One more of your suddenly furnished houses.
Eighteen years since we discovered, cash in hand,
Anonymous, the supermarket pleasures
Stacked and shinily wrapped, right
For this country, where all wipes clean,
Dries fast. Or California where you are now.

No sound from the man asleep upstairs.
At the hour's end I walk to the window
Looking over the slopes. Now the night mist
Rises off the vague plain, reaching
Our tall pine where cones cling like mussels:

Light still plays among the branches,
Touches the cold cheek of the window-pane.
I've bought blankets and firewood; we live here now.

Agello, March 1981

62

J'ai Mal à nos Dents

in memory of Anna Cullinane (Sister Mary Antony)

The Holy Father gave her leave
To return to her father's house
At seventy-eight years of age.

When she was young in the Franciscan house at Calais
She complained to the dentist, *I have a pain in our teeth*
– Her body dissolving out of her first mother,
Her five sisters aching at home.

Her brother listened to news
Five times in a morning on Radio Éireann
In Cork, as the Germans entered Calais.
Her name lay under the surface, he could not see her
Working all day with the sisters,
Stripping the hospital, loading the sick on lorries,
While Reverend Mother walked the wards and nourished them
With jugs of wine to hold their strength.
J'étais à moitié saoûle. It was done,
They lifted the old sisters on to the pig-cart
And the young walked out on the road to Desvres,
The wine still buzzing and the planes over their heads.

Je mangerai les pissenlits par les racines.
A year before she died she lost her French accent
Going home in her habit to care for her sister Nora
(Une malade à soigner une malade).
They handed her back her body,
Its voices and its death.

63

St Mary Magdalene Preaching at Marseilles

Now at the end of her life she is all hair –
A cataract flowing and freezing – and a voice
Breaking loose from the loose red hair,
The secret shroud of her skin:
A voice glittering in the wilderness.
She preaches in the city, she wanders
Late in the evening through shaded squares.

The hairs on the back of her wrists begin to lie down
And she breathes evenly, her elbows leaning
On a smooth wall. Down there in the piazza,
The boys are skimming on toy carts, warped
On their stomachs, like breathless fish.

She tucks her hair around her,
Looking beyond the game
To the suburban marshes.

Out there a shining traps the sun,
The waters are still clear,
Not a hook or a comma of ice
Holding them, the water-weeds
Lying collapsed like hair
At the turn of the tide;

They wait for the right time, then
Flip all together their thousands of sepia feet.

Chrissie

Escaped beyond hope, she climbs now
Back over the ribs of the wrecked ship,
Kneels on the crushed afterdeck, between gross
Maternal coils: the scaffolding
Surviving after pillage.
                    On the strand

The voices buzz and sink; heads can be seen
Ducking into hutches, bent over boiling pans.
The trees above the sand, like guests,
Range themselves, flounced, attentive.
Four notches down the sky, the sun gores the planks;
Light fills the growing cavity
That swells her, that ripens to her ending.

The tide returning shocks the keel;
The timbers gape again, meeting the salty breeze;
She lies where the wind rips at her left ear,
Her skirt flapping, the anchor-fluke
Biting her spine; she hears
The dull sounds from the island change
To a shrill evening cry. In her head she can see them
Pushing out boats, Mother Superior's shoulder to the stern
(Her tanned forehead more dreadful now
Than when helmeted and veiled)
                                        And she goes on fingering
In the shallow split in the wood
The grandmother's charm, a stone once shaped like a walnut,
They had never found. Salt water soaked its force:
The beat of the oars cancelled its landward grace.

She clings, as once to the horned altar beside the well.

'He Hangs in Shades the Orange Bright'

So quiet the girl in the room
                                        he says
'It is a precarious bowl
Of piled white eggs on a high shelf'

Against the dark wardrobe the gleam
Of skin and the damp hair inclining
Over her leaning shoulder fades
Into dark. She leans on a hand
Clutching the bedrail, her breasts pale

Askew as she stands looking left
Past the window towards the bright glass.
But from the window it is clear
That the dark glass reflects nothing;
Brilliance of the water-bottle
Spots the ceiling

The man in the courtyard waters the roots of the trees
And birds in their cages high on the red wall sing.

She moves her head and sees
The window tall on hinges
Each oblong tightly veiled. One side admits
Air through a grey slatted shutter, and light
Floats to the ceiling's
Profound white lake.

Still the sound of water and the stripe
Of blue sky and red wall,
Dark green leaves and fruit, one ripe orange
                                        she says
'The sheet lightning over the mountains
As I drove over the quiet plain
Past the dark orange-groves.'

She Opened the Egg

When she opened the egg the wise woman had given her,
she found inside some of her own hair and a tooth, still
bloody, from her own mouth.

One summer after another
The shore advanced and receded
As the boat shoved past the islands.

Dark bushy hills revolved in the path;
                                and in each
Of the solid still rooms above bars,
                                the first sight
Caught at an angle, the glass questioning your face.

The Bare Deal Board

I run my hand along the clean wood
And at once I am stroking the heads
Of everyone in the room.
                              Looking into the grain
Wavered and kinked like hairlines, what I see
Is the long currents of a pale ocean
Softly turning itself inside out.

Palm slack as air's belly touching the sea –
I feel the muscles tugging
In the wood, shoals hauling.

I look for that boat
Biting its groove to the south-east,
For that storm, the knot of blindness
That left us thrashing
In steel corridors in the dark.

Beyond the open window
Along the silkpacked alleys of the souq
Momentary fountains and stairways
   (My hands move over the table
   Feeling the spines of fish and the keels)
I look, and fail, in the street
Searching for a man with hair like yours.

Fireman's Lift

I was standing beside you looking up
Through the big tree of the cupola
Where the church splits wide open to admit
Celestial choirs, the fall-out of brightness.

The Virgin was spiralling to heaven,
Hauled up in stages. Past mist and shining,
Teams of angelic arms were heaving,
Supporting, crowding her, and we stepped

Back, as the painter longed to
While his arm swept in the large strokes.
We saw the work entire, and how the light

Melted and faded bodies so that
Loose feet and elbows and staring eyes
Floated in the wide stone petticoat
Clear and free as weeds.

This is what love sees, that angle:
The crick in the branch loaded with fruit,
A jaw defining itself, a shoulder yoked,

The back making itself a roof
The legs a bridge, the hands
A crane and a cradle.

Their heads bowed over to reflect on her
Fair face and hair so like their own
As she passed through their hands. We saw them
Lifting her, the pillars of their arms

(Her face a capital leaning into an arch)
As the muscles clung and shifted
For a final purchase together
Under her weight as she came to the edge of the cloud.

Parma 1963 – Dublin 1994

The Architectural Metaphor

The guide in the flashing cap explains
The lie of the land.
The buildings of the convent, founded

Here, a good mile on the safe side of the border
Before the border was changed,
Are still partly a cloister.

This was the laundry. A mountain shadow steals
Through the room, shifts by piles of folded linen.
A radio whispers behind the wall:

Since there is nothing that speaks as clearly
As music, no other voice that says
Hold me I'm going . . . so faintly,

Now light scatters, a door opens, laughter breaks in,
A young girl barefoot, a man pushing her
Backwards against the hatch –

It flies up suddenly –
There lies the foundress, pale
In her funeral sheets, her face turned west

Searching for the rose-window. It shows her
What she never saw from any angle but this:
Weeds nested in the churchyard, catching the late sun,

Herself at fourteen stumbling downhill
And landing, and crouching to watch
The sly limbering of the bantam hen

Foraging between gravestones –
                                        Help is at hand
Though out of reach:
                          The world not dead after all.

  1989

  69

The Real Thing

The Book of Exits, miraculously copied
Here in this convent by an angel's hand,
Stands open on a lectern, grooved
Like the breast of a martyred deacon.

The bishop has ordered the windows bricked up on this side
Facing the fields beyond the city.
Lit by the glow from the cloister yard at noon
On Palm Sunday, Sister Custos
Exposes her major relic, the longest
Known fragment of the Brazen Serpent.

True stories wind and hang like this
Shuddering loop wreathed on a lapis lazuli
Frame. She says, this is the real thing.
She veils it again and locks up.
On the shelves behind her the treasures are lined.
The episcopal seal repeats every coil,
Stamped on all closures of each reliquary
Where the labels read: *Bones*
Of Different Saints. Unknown.

Her history is a blank sheet,
Her vows a folded paper locked like a well.
The torn end of the serpent
Tilts the lace edge of the veil.
The real thing, the one free foot kicking
Under the white sheet of history.

The Water Journey

I sent the girl to the well.
She walked up the main road as far as Tell's Cross,
Turned left over the stile and up the hill path.
I stood at the door to watch her coming down,
Her eyes fixed on the level of the water
Cushioned in her palms, wavering
Like the circles of grain in wood.

She stepped neatly down the road;
The lads on bicycles cheered as they passed her
And her fingers shook and nearly leaked and lost it.
She took her time for the last fifty yards
Bringing it to the threshold and there I drank.

I said to the other sisters, each of you
Will have to do the same when your day comes.
This one has finished her turn,
She can go home with her wages;
She would hardly make it as far
As the well at the world's end.

Saint Margaret of Cortona

Patroness of the Lock Hospital, Townsend Street, Dublin

She had become, the preacher hollows his voice,
A name not to be spoken, the answer
To the witty man's loose riddle, what's she
That's neither maiden, widow nor wife?

A pause opens its jaws
In the annual panegyric,
The word *whore* prowling silent
Up and down the long aisle.

Under the flourishing canopy
Where trios of angels mime the last trombone,
Behind the silver commas of the shrine,
In the mine of the altar her teeth listen and smile.

She is still here, she refuses
To be consumed. The weight of her bones
Burns down through the mountain.
Her death did not make her like this;

Her eyes were hollowed
By the bloody scene: the wounds
In the body of her child's father
Tumbled in a ditch. The door was locked,
The names flew and multiplied; she turned
Her back but the names clustered and hung
Out of her shoulderbones
Like children swinging from a father's arm,
Their tucked-up feet skimming over the ground.

Our Lady of Youghal

Flowing and veiling and peeled back, the tide
Washed the bulk of timber
Beached on the mud, so heavy
Twelve horses could not pull it.

A lay brother rose at dawn, and saw it moved,
The weight melted away,
To the shore below the water-gate.
He rolled it easily as far as the cloister.

At rest on the lip of weathered
Rough steps and the icy pavement,
It paused among the kneeling poor
The bark still crude and whole.

It takes the blind man's fingers
Blessing himself in the entry
To find the secret water treasured
In the tree's elbow; he washes his eyes and sees
A leaf cutting its way to the air
Inside a tower of leaves,
The virgin's almond shrine, its ivory lids parting
Behind lids of gold, bursting out of the wood.

Following

So she follows the trail of her father's coat through the fair
Shouldering past beasts packed solid as books,
And the dealing men nearly as slow to give way –
A block of a belly, a back like a mountain,
A shifting elbow like a plumber's bend –
When she catches a glimpse of a shirt-cuff, a handkerchief,
Then the hard brim of his hat, skimming along,

Until she is tracing light footsteps
Across the shivering bog by starlight,
The dead corpse risen from the wakehouse
Gliding before her in a white habit.
The ground is forested with gesturing trunks,
Hands of women dragging needles,
Half-choked heads in the water of cuttings,
Mouths that roar like the noise of the fair day.

She comes to where he is seated
With whiskey poured out in two glasses
In a library where the light is clean,
His clothes all finely laundered,
Ironed facings and linings.
The smooth foxed leaf has been hidden
In a forest of fine shufflings,
The square of white linen
That held three drops
Of her heart's blood is shelved

Between the gatherings
That go to make a book –
The crushed flowers among the pages crack
The spine open, push the bindings apart.

Woman Shoeing a Horse

This is the path to the stile
And this is where I would stand –
The place is all thick with weeds.

I could see the line of her back and the flash of her hair
As she came from the fields at a call,
And then ten minutes wasted, all quiet

But the horse in the open air clanking his feet
Until the fire was roaring and the work began,
And the clattering and dancing.

I could see by her shoulders how her breath shifted
In the burst of heat, and the wide gesture of her free arm
As she lifted the weight and clung

Around the hoof. The hammer notes were flying
All urgent with fire and speed, and precise
With a finicky catch at the end –

But the noise I could not hear was the shock of air
Crashing into her lungs, the depth
Of the gasp as she turned with a ready hand

As the heat from the fire drew up the chimney,
The flame pressing, brushing out the last thread,
Constantly revising itself upwards to a pure line.

I closed my eyes, not to see the rider as he left.
When I opened them again the sheep were inching forward,
A flock of starlings had darkened the sky.

Vierge Ouvrante

Overhead on the ladder
A craftsman can be heard ascending
Balancing the hammer and nails.

He tacks up the photographs:
How can he hold in his head all the leaves of that tree
Whose roots are everywhere, whose seed
Outnumbers the spawn of the ocean?

The woman in an anorak, snapped
Face down in a drain, her bare arse
Signalling to helicopters, hardly
Finds room beside the man boldly
Laid out on the stone slab
As naked as an elephant.

Mercifully in the last room
Cameras are not allowed.
You have to do your best with glass and shadows
And the light shining along the passages of your skull
To capture her, to remember

The opening virgin, her petticoats
Shelved like the poplars of an avenue
That slip aside until she uncovers the scars,
The marks of the ropes that chafed and held her
So she could not move or write but only commit
To the long band of memory that bound her like a
    silkworm's thread
The tearing, the long falling, the splashing and staining
    she saw.
And as she unwinds she begins to spin like a dancer
    against the clock
And in one minute the room is full of the stuff, sticky,
White as a blue-bleached sheet in the sun –
Till there is nothing left of the darkness you need
For the *camera oscura*,
Only the shining of the blank chronicle of thread.

75

Man Watching a Woman

The sound of everything folding into sleep,
A sense of being nowhere at all,
Set him on his way (traffic far off, and wind
In tall trees) to a back gate, a dark yard.
A path goes past the bins, the kitchen door,
Switches to a gravel walk by the windows
Lit softly above the privet hedge.
He stops and watches. He needs to see this:

A woman working late in the refectory,
Sewing a curtain, the lines of her face
Dropping into fatigue, severity, age,
The hair falling out of its clasp at her poll.
The hands are raised to thread the needle,
The tongue moves behind her lips.
He cannot see the feet or shoes, they are trapped
In toils of cloth. He is comforted.

He can move on, while the night combs out
Long rushing sounds into quiet,
On to the scene, the wide cafés –
Trombone music over polished tables.
He will watch the faces behind the bar, tired girls,
Their muscles bracing under breakers of music
And the weight of their balancing trays, drinks, ice and change.

That Summer

So what did she do that summer
When they were all out working?

If she moved she felt a soft rattle
That settled like a purseful of small change.
She staggered through the quiet of the house,
Leaned on a flowering doorpost
And went back inside from the glare
Feeling in her skirt pocket the skin on her hands,
Never so smooth since her fourteenth year.

One warm evening they were late;
She walked across the yard with a can,
Watered a geranium and kept on going
Till she came to the ridge looking over the valley
At the low stacked hills, the steep ground
Between that plunged like a funnel of sand.
She couldn't face back home, they came for her
As she stood watching the hills breathing out and in,
Their dialogue of hither and yon.

A Hand, A Wood

1

After three days I have to wash –
I am prising you from under my nails
Reluctantly, as time will deface
The tracks, their branching sequence,
The skill of the left and the right hand.

Your script curls on the labels of jars,
Naming pulses in the kitchen press.
The dates you marked in the diary come and pass.

2

The wet leaves are blowing, the sparse
Ashes are lodged under the trees in the wood
Where we cannot go in this weather.
The stream is full and rattling,
The hunters are scattering shot –
The birds fly up and spread out.

I am wearing your shape
Like a light shirt of flame;
My hair is full of shadows.

Studying the Language

On Sundays I watch the hermits coming out of their holes
Into the light. Their cliff is as full as a hive.
They crowd together on warm shoulders of rock
Where the sun has been shining, their joints crackle.
They begin to talk after a while.
I listen to their accents, they are not all
From this island, not all old,
Not even, I think, all masculine.

They are so wise, they do not pretend to see me.
They drink from the scattered pools of melted snow:
I walk right by them and drink when they have done.
I can see the marks of chains around their feet.

I call this my work, these decades and stations –
Because, without these, I would be a stranger here.

The Girl Who Married the Reindeer

1

When she came to the finger-post
She turned right and walked as far as the mountains.

Patches of snow lay under the thorny bush
That was blue with sloes. She filled her pockets.
The sloes piled into the hollows of her skirt.
The sunset wind blew cold against her belly
And light shrank between the branches
While her feet shifted, bare,
While her hands raked in the hard fruit.

The reindeer halted before her and claimed the sloes.
She rode home on his back without speaking,
Holding her rolled-up skirt,
Her free hand grasping the wide antlers
To keep her steady on the long ride.

2

Thirteen months after she left home
She travelled hunched on the deck of a trader
Southwards to her sister's wedding.

Her eyes reflected acres of snow,
Her breasts were large from suckling,
There was salt in her hair.

They met her staggering on the quay;
They put her in a scented bath,
Found a silk dress, combed her hair out.

How could they let her go back to stay
In that cold house with that strange beast?
So the old queen said, the bridegroom's mother.

They slipped a powder in her drink,
So she forgot her child, her friend,
The snow and the sloe gin.

3

The reindeer died when his child was ten years old.
Naked in death his body was a man's,
Young, with an old man's face and scored with grief.

When the old woman felt his curse she sickened,
She lay in her tower bedroom and could not speak.
The young woman who had nursed her grandchildren
    nursed her.

In her witch time she could not loose her spells
Or the spells of time, though she groaned for power.
The nurse went downstairs to sit in the sun. She slept.
The child from the north was heard at the gate.

4

Led by the migrating swallows
The boy from the north stood in the archway
That looked into the courtyard where water fell,
His arm around the neck of his companion –
A wild reindeer staggered by sunlight.
His hair was bleached, his skin blistered.
He saw the woman in wide silk trousers
Come out of the door at the foot of the stair,
Sit on a cushion, and stretch her right hand for a hammer.
She hammered the dried broad beans one by one,
While the swallows timed her, swinging side to side:
The hard skin fell away, and the left hand
Tossed the bean into the big brass pot.
It would surely take her all day to do them all.
Her face did not change though she saw the child watching.

A light wind fled over them
As the witch died in the high tower.
She knew her child in that moment:
His body poured into her vision
Like a snake pouring over the ground,
Like a double-mouthed fountain of two nymphs,
The light groove scored on his chest
Like the meeting of two tidal roads, two oceans.

Bessboro

This is what I inherit –
It was never my own life,
But a house's name I heard
And others heard as warning
Of what might happen a girl
Daring and caught by ill-luck:
A fragment of desolate
Fact, a hammer-note of fear –

But I never saw the place.
Now that I stand at the gate
And that time is so long gone
It is their absence that rains,
That stabs right into the seams
Of my big coat, settling
On my shoulder, a pointed
Shower, crowding the short day.

The white barred gate is closed,
The white fence tracks out of sight
Where the avenue goes, rain
Veils distance, dimming all sound
And a halfdrawn lace of mist
Hides elements of the known:
Gables and high blind windows.
The story has moved away.

The rain darns into the grass,
Blown over the tidal lough
Past the isolated roof
And the tall trees in the park;
It gusts off to south and west;
Earth is secret as ever:
The blood that was sown here flowered
And all the seeds blew away.

Translation

For the reburial of the Magdalens.

The soil frayed and sifted evens the score –
There are women here from every county,
Just as there were in the laundry.

White light blinded and bleached out
The high relief of a glance, where steam danced
Around stone drains and giggled and slipped across water.

Assist them now, ridges under the veil, shifting,
Searching for their parents, their names,
The edges of words grinding against nature,

As if, when water sank between the rotten teeth
Of soap, and every grasp seemed melted, one voice
Had begun, rising above the shuffle and hum

Until every pocket in her skull blared with the note –
Allow us now to hear it, sharp as an infant's cry
While the grass takes root, while the steam rises:

> Washed clean of idiom: the baked crust
> Of words that made my temporary name:
> A parasite that grew in me: that spell
> Lifted: I lie in earth sifted to dust:
> Let the bunched keys I bore slacken and fall:
> I rise and forget: a cloud over my time.

An Alcove

What is it, in the air or the walls
Hunched over me, defending
The stiffbacked chairs caught off guard
And the knitting cramped in its bag
On the low shelf by the dead fire?
The stray cat's tail twitches on the windowsill,
The garden is a patch of frozen grass.

In these rooms every stitch, step and
Edge of a tile is the same age, is wearing
Away at the same rate, like an old lady
Who brings out the sherry because tea means trouble
But has not barred her door.

There are porched crannies, for waiting in while the
    doctor is with her
And the kind of book one reads in such emergencies,
With mauve and brown pictures, Paolo and Francesca
Coiled like the wisteria's double trunk
In the one safe place, an alcove in the wind.

Medbh McGuckian

Smoke

They set the whins on fire along the road.
I wonder what controls it, can the wind hold
That snake of orange motion to the hills,
Away from the houses?

They seem so sure what they can do.
I am unable even
To contain myself, I run
Till the fawn smoke settles on the earth.

Mr McGregor's Garden

Some women save their sanity with needles.
I complicate my life with studies
Of my favourite rabbit's head, his vulgar volatility,
Or a little ladylike sketching
Of my resident toad in his flannel box;
Or search for handsome fungi for my tropical
Herbarium, growing dry-rot in the garden,
And wishing that the climate were kinder,
Turning over the spiky purple heads among the moss
With my cheese-knife to view the slimy veil.

Unlike the cupboard-love of sleepers in the siding,
My hedgehog's sleep is under his control
And not the weather's; he can rouse himself
At half-an-hour's notice in the frost, or leave at will
On a wet day in August, by the hearth.
He goes by breathing slowly, after a large meal,
A lively evening, very cross if interrupted,
And returns with a hundred respirations
To the minute, weak and nervous when he wakens,
Busy with his laundry.

On sleepless nights while learning
Shakespeare off by heart,
I feel that Bunny's at my bedside
In a white cotton nightcap,
Tickling me with his whiskers.

Slips

The studied poverty of a moon roof,
The earthenware of dairies cooled by apple trees,
The apple tree that makes the whitest wash . . .

But I forget names, remembering them wrongly
Where they touch upon another name,
A town in France like a woman's Christian name.

My childhood is preserved as a nation's history,
My favourite fairytales the shells
Leased by the hermit crab.

I see my grandmother's death as a piece of ice,
My mother's slimness restored to her,
My own key slotted in your door –

Tricks you might guess from this unfastened button,
A pen mislaid, a word misread,
My hair coming down in the middle of a conversation.

The Sofa

Do not be angry if I tell you
Your letter stayed unopened on my table
For several days. If you were friend enough
To believe me, I was about to start writing
At any moment; my mind was savagely made up,
Like a serious sofa moved
Under a north window. My heart, alas,

Is not the calmest of places.
Still it is not my heart that needs replacing:
And my books seem real enough to me,
My disasters, my surrenders, all my loss. . . .
Since I was child enough to forget
That you loathe poetry, you ask for some –
About nature, greenery, insects, and, of course,

The sun – surely that would be to open
An already open window? To celebrate
The impudence of flowers? If I could
Interest you instead in his large, gentle stares,
How his soft shirt is the inside of pleasure
To me, why I must wear white for him,
Imagine he no longer trembles

When I approach, no longer buys me
Flowers for my name day. . .. But I spread
On like a house, I begin to scatter
To a tiny to-and-fro at odds
With the wear on my threshold. Somewhere
A curtain rising wonders where I am,
My books sleep, pretending to forget me.

To My Grandmother

I would revive you with a swallow's nest:
For as long a time as I could hold my breath
I would feel your pulse like tangled weeds
Separate into pearls. The heart should rule
The summer, ringing like a sickle over
The need to make life hard. I would
Sedate your eyes with rippleseed, those
Hollow points that close as if
Your eyelids had been severed
To deny you sleep, imagine you a dawn.
I would push a chrysanthemum stone
Into your sleeve without your noticing
Its reaching far, its going, its returning.
When the end of summer comes, it is
A season by itself; when your tongue
Curls back like a sparrow's buried head,
I would fill your mouth with rice and mussels.

Gateposts

A man will keep a horse for prestige,
But a woman ripens best underground.
He settles where the wind
Brings his whirling hat to rest,
And the wind decides which door is to be used.

Under the hip-roofed thatch,
The bed-wing is warmed by the chimney breast;
On either side the keeping-holes
For his belongings, hers.

He says it's unlucky to widen the house
And leaves the gateposts holding up the fairies.
He lays his lazy-beds and burns the river,
He builds turf-castles,
And sprigs the corn with apple-mint.

She spreads heather on the floor
And sifts the oatmeal ark for thin-bread farls:
All through the blue month, July,
She tosses stones in basins to the sun,
And watches for the trout in the holy well.

The Flower Master

Like foxgloves in the school of the grass moon
We come to terms with shade, with the principle
Of enfolding space. Our scissors in brocade,
We learn the coolness of straight edges, how
To stroke gently the necks of daffodils
And make them throw their heads back to the sun.

We slip the thready stems of violets, delay
The loveliness of the hibiscus dawn with quiet ovals,
Spirals of feverfew like water splashing,
The papery legacies of bluebells. We do
Sea-fans with sea-lavender, moon-arrangements
Roughly for the festival of moon-viewing.

This black container calls for sloes, sweet
Sultan, dainty nipplewort, in honour
Of a special guest who, summoned to the
Tea ceremony, must stoop to our low doorway,
Our fontanelle, the trout's dimpled feet.

The Moon Pond

I thought this morning of my yellowed Juliette cap,
Its head-dress of artificial pearls that I wore once,
And never wore again. . ... It is not the same
With this bright moon pond where, they say,
If you come once you'll likely come again,
Fed slowly by the natural canal, where the otter swims
You dreamt had made you pregnant.

As with an egg I close my mouth, with an egg
I open it again, my May Day rising, after
My warrior's sleep, and crossing the fat churchyard
Left by a green Christmas, the souls of the dead
As thick as bees in an uncut meadow round me.
I leave a bowl of spring water womanly on the table
For your wild and nameless sprays before they withered.

I leave a stack of salt fallen from a thimble,
A measure of milk with a cock's step of butter,
Coming in hills and going in mountains:
For this milk-fevered lady is the round-eyed child
Listening with bated breath to the singalong
Of birds that, waking in the heart of rain,
Would just as boldly start to mate again.

The Aphrodisiac

She gave it out as if it were
A marriage or a birth, some other
Interesting family event, that she
Had finished sleeping with him, that
Her lover was her friend. It was his heart
She wanted, the bright key to his study,
Not the menacings of love. So he is
Banished to his estates, to live
Like a man in a glasshouse; she has taken to
A little cap of fine white lace
In the mornings, feeds her baby
In a garden you could visit blindfold
For its scent alone:
                              But though a ray of grace
Has fallen, all her books seem as frumpish
As the last year's gambling game, when she
Would dress in pink taffeta, and drive
A blue phaeton, or in blue, and drive
A pink one, with her black hair supported
By a diamond comb, floating about
Without panniers. How his most
Caressing look, his husky whisper suffocates her,
This almost perfect power of knowing
More than a kept woman. The between-maid
Tells me this is not the only secret staircase.
Rumour has it she's taken to rouge again.

The Flitting

'You wouldn't believe all this house has cost me –
In body-language terms, it has turned me upside down.'
I've been carried from one structure to the other
On a chair of human arms, and liked the feel
Of being weightless, that fraternity of clothes. . . .
Now my own life hits me in the throat, the bumps
And cuts of the walls as telling
As the poreholes in strawberries, tomato seeds.
I cover them for safety with these Dutch girls
Making lace, or leaning their almond faces
On their fingers with a mandolin, a dreamy
Chapelled ease abreast this other turquoise-turbanned,
Glancing over her shoulder with parted mouth.

She seems a garden escape in her unconscious
Solidarity with darkness, clove-scented
As an orchid taking fifteen years to bloom,
And turning clockwise as the honeysuckle.
Who knows what importance
She attaches to the hours?
Her narrative secretes its own values, as mine might
If I painted the half of me that welcomes death
In a faggotted dress, in a peacock chair,
No falser biography than our casual talk
Of losing a virginity, or taking a life, and
No less poignant if dying
Should consist in more than waiting.

I postpone my immortality for my children,
Little rock-roses, cushioned
In long-flowering sea-thrift and metrics,
Lacking elemental memories:
I am well-earthed here as the digital clock,
Its numbers flicking into place like overgrown farthings
On a bank where once a train
Ploughed like an emperor living out a myth
Through the cambered flesh of clover and wild carrot.

From the Dressing-Room

Left to itself, they say, every foetus
Would turn female, staving in, nature
Siding then with the enemy that
Delicately mixes up genders. This
Is an absence I have passionately sought,
Brightening nevertheless my poet's attic
With my steady hands, calling him my blue
Lizard till his moans might be heard
At the far end of the garden. For I like
His ways, he's light on his feet and does
Not break anything, puts his entire soul
Into bringing me a glass of water.

I can take anything now, even his being
Away, for it always seems to me his
Writing is for me, as I walk springless
From the dressing-room in a sisterly
Length of flesh-coloured silk. Oh there
Are moments when you think you can
Give notice in a jolly, wifely tone,
Tossing off a very last and sunsetty
Letter of farewell, with strict injunctions
To be careful to procure his own lodgings,
That my good little room is lockable,
But shivery, I recover at the mere
Sight of him propping up my pillow.

On Not Being Your Lover

Your eyes were ever brown, the colour
Of time's submissiveness. Love nerves
Or a heart, beat in their world of
Privilege, I had not yet kissed you
On the mouth.

But I would not say, in my un-freedom
I had weakly drifted there, like the
Bone-deep blue that visits and decants
The eyes of our children:

How warm and well-spaced their dreams
You can tell from the sleep-late mornings
Taken out of my face! Each lighted
Window shows me cardiganed, more desolate
Than the garden, and more hallowed
Than the hinge of the brass-studded
Door that we close, and no one opens,
That we open and no one closes.

In a far-flung, too young part,
I remembered all your slender but
Persistent volume said, friendly, complex
As the needs of your new and childfree girl.

Prie-Dieu

Although my dresser still contains
Christmas cards in May, I have ceased
To send the bluebelled notelets mourning
The world that is dead in me, my mother's
Sleeping-hide. It seems at last
My upright chair beside a separate
Fireplace can cope as well
As any honest woman with the rage
Of one moment, the contentment of the next.

You see me all untutored, always
Sexed, a postulant that will not kiss
Until the clothing ceremony. Yet
This oblique trance is my natural
Way of speaking, I have jilted
All the foursquare houses, and
My courtyard has a Spanish air,
Defiant as a tomboy; under the pelmet
And the reading lamp, the white
St Joseph, a bunch of flowers
Clearly gathered by a child.

Venus and the Rain

White on white, I can never be viewed
Against a heavy sky – my gibbous voice
Passes from leaf to leaf, retelling the story
Of its own provocative fractures, till
Their facing coasts might almost fill each other
And they ask me in reply if I've
Decided to stop trying to make diamonds.

On one occasion, I rang like a bell
For a whole month, promising their torn edges
The birth of a new ocean (as all of us
Who have hollow bodies tend to do at times):
What clues to distance could they have,
So self-excited by my sagging sea,
Widening ten times faster than it really did?

Whatever rivers sawed their present lairs
Through my lightest, still-warm rocks,
I told them they were only giving up
A sun for sun, that cruising moonships find
Those icy domes relaxing, when they take her
Rind to pieces, and a waterfall
Unstitching itself down the front stairs.

What Does 'Early' Mean?

Happy house across the road
My eighteen-inch deep study of you
Is like a chair carried out into the garden,
And back again because the grass is wet.

Yet I think winter has ended
Privately in you, and lies in half-sleep,
Or her last sleep, at the foot
Of one of your mirrors – hence
The spring-day smile with which
You smarten up your mouth
Into a retina of new roofs, new thoughts.

None of my doors has slammed
Like that, every sentence is the same
Old workshop sentence, ending
Rightly or wrongly in the ruins
Of an evening spent in puzzling
Over the meaning of six o'clock or seven:

Or why the house across the road
Has such a moist-day sort of name,
Evoking ships and their wind-blown ways.

A Conversation Set to Flowers

That fine china we conceived in spring
And lost in summer has blown the final crumbs
Out of the book I was reading. Though one
Is still bending over prams, an ice-blue peak
Over the frills of houses.

The dress of ecru lace you bought me
At the February sales is still all heart.
I cup my hands, thin as a window-pane
Unevenly blown, as if to hold
Some liquid in my palm, and the rings
Slide up and down.

In my birth-dreams light falls in pleats
Or steps, the room after those terrible attacks
Is a white forest, scented with sea,
And we both change into apples, my breasts
And knees into apples, though you
Are more apple than they could possibly be.

But what the snow said, long ago,
To the grey north door and the short day,
Breaks through like the multi-coloured
Sunrise round a stamp on a letter:
A hill-wind blows at the book's edges
To open a page.

Sea or Sky?

Small doses, effleurage will do,
Because I never garden. Wednesday comes
Out of the rim of bones with a port-wine
Stain on its face, a day of possible
Excitements, no sky, yet you know immediately
The colour it should be. I play it down,
The agitated sky of my choice, I assume
That echo of light over there is the sun
Improperly burning. In a sea of like mood
A wave is trying to break, to give a reason
For water striking something else, and the grey
Below the wave is a darker version
Of the moisture-laden sky I should be working in.
(Not the clear water of your sleep where you
Seem lighter, and the garden's voice has gone inside.)

The athletic anatomy of waves, in their
Reflectiveness, rebirth, means my new, especially
Dense breasts can be touched, can be
Uplifted from the island of burned skin
Where my heart used to be, now I'm
Seeing eyes that, sea or sky, have seen you.

Minus 18 Street

I never loved you more
Than when I let you sleep another hour,
As if you intended to make such a gate of time
Your home. Speechless as night animals,
The breeze and I breakfasted
With the pure desire of speech; but let
Each petal of your dream have its chance,
The many little shawls that covered you:

I never envied your child's face
Its motherless cheekbones, or sensed in them
The approach of illness – how you were being
Half-killed on a sea-shore, or falling
From a ladder where you knelt to watch
The quartering of the moon. (You would never
Swim to the top of the rain that bathed
The mute world of her body.)

Sleep for you is a trick
Of the frost, a light green room in a French house,
Giving no trouble till spring.
The wedding-boots of the wind
Blow footsteps behind me,
I count each season for the sign
Of wasted children.

Sky of blue water, blue-water sky,
I sleep with the dubious kiss
Of my sky-blue portfolio.
Under or over the wind,
In soft and independent clothes,
I begin each dawn-coloured picture
Deep in your snow.

Four O'Clock, Summer Street

As a child cries, all over, I kept insisting
On robin's egg blue tiles around the fireplace,
Which gives a room a kind of flying-heartedness.

Only that tiny slice of the house absorbed
My perfume – like a kiss sliding off into
A three-sided mirror – like a red-brown girl

In cuffless trousers we add to ourselves by looking.
She had the boy-girl body of a flower,
Moving once and for all past the hermetic front door.

I knew she was drinking blue and it had dried
In her; she carried it wide awake in herself
Ever after, and its music blew that other look

To bits. If what she hunted for could fit my eyes,
I would shine in the window of her blood like wine,
Or perfume, or till nothing was left of me but listening.

Little House, Big House

In a day or two the chairs will fall to pieces:
Those who were once lovers need the minimum
Of furniture, half-people, each with his separate sky.

Christmas peered through the escallonia hedge,
And passed almost unnoticed, except the stamps
Had squirrels on them. Why should I take
My apron off for a wineless dinner? My things
Are too grey, like a tree I deepen shadows
With my brown autumn raincoat.

On the ground floor, one room opens into another,
And a small Matisse in the inglenook
Without its wood fire is stroked by light
From north and south. That started all the feelings
That had slept till then, I came out
From behind the tea-pot to find myself
Cooled by a new arrangement of doorways
And choosing a spiced bun from a china shell.

A shawl no whiter than my white skin
Made me a dust-jacket, I overwatered
The Michaelmas daisies thinking about
The claw-like bedroom door-handles along
The minstrel's gallery. And the house like me
Was tangled with the emotion of cut flowers –

So different from an ordinary going-away –
That I could hardly keep my hand
From phoning you, impromptu. Since our blood
Is always older than we will ever be,
I should like to lie in Tarusa under matted winter grass,
Where the strawberries are redder than anything else.

The Dream-Language of Fergus

1

Your tongue has spent the night
in its dim sack as the shape of your foot
in its cave. Not the rudiment
of half a vanquished sound,
the excommunicated shadow of a name,
has rumpled the sheets of your mouth.

2

So Latin sleeps, they say, in Russian speech,
so one river inserted into another
becomes a leaping, glistening, splashed
and scattered alphabet
jutting out from the voice,
till what began as a dog's bark
ends with bronze, what began
with honey ends with ice;
as if an aeroplane in full flight
launched a second plane,
the sky is stabbed by their exits
and the mistaken meaning of each.

3

Conversation is as necessary
among these familiar campus trees
as the apartness of torches;
and if I am a threader
of double-stranded words, whose
Quando has grown into now,
no text can return the honey
in its path of light from a jar,
only a seed-fund, a pendulum,
pressing out the diasporic snow.

Gigot Sleeves

There are bibles left about the house:
Here is the bible open, here is the bible shut,
A spreading here, a condensation there.

The double-cherry performs a dance behind
Triple gauze, she takes out the bulldogs,
Masters a pistol, sleeps on a camp bed

Without a fireplace or curtain, in the
Narrow sliproom over the front hall –
A woman-sized, un-beringed, inexact fit.

When she hears the wheels of his carriage,
She blows out the candle, she does not yearn
For the company of even a lamp.

For a gown-length, she chooses
A book-muslin patterned with lilac
Thunder and lightning. Her skirts

Are splashed with purple suns, the sleeves
Set in as they used to be fifteen years
Ago. If she takes up a piece of sewing,

She will be shirt-making; in a laundry-book
She writes as though fifteen hundred Englishmen
Had been slaughtered just beyond the garden,

Or it was there Trelawney threw the frankincense
And salt into the fire, poured the wine
And oil over the wave-worn depths of Shelley.

Her petticoats have neither curve nor wave
In them, the whole depth of the house,
Like a secret tie between a wound and its weapon.

And everything is emaciated – the desk
On her knees, the square of carpet, the black
Horsehair sofa, and the five-foot-seven by sixteen

Inches, a pair of months, stopped.

The Most Emily of All

When you dream wood I dream water.
When you dream boards, or cupboard,
I dream a lake of rain, a race sprung
From the sea. If you call out 'house' to me
And I answer 'library', you answer me
By the very terms of your asking,
As a sentence clings tighter
Because it makes no sense.

Your light hat with the dark band
Keeps turning up; you pull it right
Down over your head and run the fingers
Of your right hand up and down
In a groove on the door panel. A finger
Going like this into my closed hand
Feels how my line of life turns back
Upon itself, in the kind of twilight
Before the moon is seen.

A verse from a poem by Lermentov
Continually goes round
In my head. A full ten days
Has elapsed since I started my
'You can go or stay' letter, increasingly
Without lips like the moon that night,
A repercussive mouth made for nothing,
And used for nothing.
Just let me moisten your dreamwork
With the lower half of the letter,
Till my clove-brown eyes beget a taller blue.

Breaking the Blue

Deluged with the dustless air, unspeaking likeness:
You, who were the spaces between words in the act of reading,
A colour sewn on to colour, break the blue.

Single version of my mind deflected off my body,
Side-altar, sacramental, tasting-table, leaf to my
Emptying shell, heart with its aortic opening,

Your mouth, my dress was the scene that framed
Your eye shut like hands or hair, we coiled
In the lifelong snake of sleep, we poised together

Against the crevice formed by death's forefinger
And thumb, where her shoulder splits when desire
Goes further than the sender will allow.

Womb-encased and ever-present mystery without
Release, your even-coloured foliage seems a town garden
To my inaccessible, severely mineral world.

Fragments of once-achieved meaning, ready to leave
The flesh, re-integrate as lover, mother, words
That overwhelm me: You utter, become music, are played.

Clotho

Music is my heroine, the synthetic kisses
Of a woman's body. Drop by drop
She distilled them, I watched the non-togetherness
Of her sweetish old-maid lips,
Her trained and pocket-mouthed smile.

Like the shadow of an aeroplane
With but one side of wings,
She moved parallel to me,
Leaving the air unflown.

My arms were stretched as high
And wide as they could go,
A distaff reaching from heaven to earth.
But there was nothing to burn
My tongue on, not even a broken stalk
Of lilac-veined sound behind her broken eyes.

Blue does not describe them, they were
A blue and silver room
They sent me half-filled away.
I dropped three-quarters
Of my words for I did not need them.

They should be another colour,
There should be black swans,
Though a satellite is never
Anything but feminine, and crawls
Under your pillow
Because of the horror of touch.

There should be a darkness
Which is anything but death,
Not the false daylight of the stage,
The most expensive white
Of all those pairs of hands
Born for a few sealed railway trains,
All of which were dead by morning.

In just these moments it has grown dark,
And the moon, the semi-human,
Radioactive moon, is at a diagonal
Past childbearing, neither lying down
Nor sitting, since this
Is a flowerless month.

I am possessed of such strength
That I knock down my servant,
My house god, my all-powerful
Mistress of tone, and her moan
Comes clear-cut from another world,
As if translating.

The Partner's Desk

Yesterday was a gift, a copy of the afternoon,
A heavily wrapped book, a rolled manuscript.
Its paper was buff with blue lines, the sheets
Ragged at the top, and not quite legal size.
It was secured on three sides by green ribbons
Like a wooden tongue of land or the leafy miles
Of a ribbon-maker and, whether it was a letter
He withheld from me, I swore to seal it through death.

The colour is deep enough by itself to make
The children pray for the dead; it is a children's morning.
I arranged the Christmas tree in its green outfit,
Producing its green against the grey sky like handwriting
That has been traced over or, when snow tires us,
The sunshine inside and out of my birthday dove.
Both our birthdays are today, and I was playing with
Its feather on the bed as if it were a brake

On the thawing weather, that almost-summer
Had already arrived. Being still in the grip
Of a dream of pearls which robbed me
Of my un-English language (yesterday
He dreamed of laburnums). It is December,
Though the wine is May's, and we should keep birds
Only in winter, as we burn the winter
In our curse-laden, extinguished Christmas tree.

Everything I do passes through a narrow door,
And the door seems rather heavy. When I play
The piano my eyes turn brown; it is not a matter
Of eyes, it is something darker than eye-colour,
And we are all part of it. When I teach the continents
To my favourite daughter, my father is there
Though I do not see him. His mood is towards evening.
He asks the bird how many years he has to live,

110

Or how long the hours will continue to strike.
How very deliberately the bird breaks off,
Praising the stillness. He compares this cry
With his outward appearance, he strokes the veins
On the back of his left hand and extends
His fingers, he looks up at the ceiling
And down at the floor, he feels in his breast
Pocket and pulls a green pamphlet out,

Saying, 'The finest summer I can ever remember
Produced you,' and I remember a second,
Gentler dream, of my wedding year,
Where we took a walk across loose stones,
And he took my hands and stretched them out
As if I were on a cross, but not being punished.
You know the renewed rousing of your fingers
In a dream, your hand glides through the air,

They are not fingers at all. He will leave me
The school clock, the partner's desk, the hanging
Lamp, the head bearing the limbs, as I will leave her
The moonphase watch and the bud vase. I restart
My diary and reconstruct the days. I look upon
The life-bringing cloud as cardboard
And no reason for the life of another soul, yet still
Today is the true midsummer day.

Marconi's Cottage

Small and watchful as a lighthouse,
A pure clear place of no particular childhood,
It is as if the sea had spoken in you
And then the words had dried.

Bitten and fostered by the sea
And by the British spring,
There seems only this one way of happening,
And a poem to prove it has happened.

Now I am close enough, I open my arms
To your castle-thick walls, I must learn
To use your wildness when I lock and unlock
Your door weaker than kisses.

Maybe you are a god of sorts,
Or a human star, lasting in spite of us
Like a note propped against a bowl of flowers,
Or a red shirt to wear against light blue.

The bed of your mind has weathered
Books of love, you are all I have gathered
To me of otherness; the worn glisten
Of your flesh is relearned and reloved.

Another unstructured, unmarried, unfinished
Summer, slips its unclenched weather
Into my winter poems, cheating time
And blood of their timelessness.

Let me have you for what we call
Forever, the deeper opposite of a picture,
Your leaves, the part of you
That the sea first talked to.

Candles at Three Thirty

The year fades without ripening,
but glitters as it withers
like an orange stuck with cloves
or Christmas clouds.

Bits of very new,
dream-quilted sky
are touched to an arrangement,
all but kiss.

Dark blue gathers around the waist
into a humbler colour;
two cottages flush with the road
slowly edge back.

When I am all harbour, ask too much,
go up like the land
to points and precipices,
meanwhile is my anchor.

The island with its quick primrose light
turns aside and walks away
from my swollen shadows,
but carries the road southwards.

Frail as tobacco flowers,
a featherweight seagull
still damp on my brocade curtain
is ready for sea again.

A meaningless white thread
of pale travel-sleep
rippling one side only
of his unlighted eyes,

intelligent and soulless,
sees everybody happening
as down a warmed room.
The upper half of the house made fast,

we try to batten the door-windows,
but one won't fasten,
the thin edge of the sea's blade
curves around its oak, rustless as flesh.

Out between the rosemary hedges,
sky and sea part in a long
mauve-silver tress
like an oyster shell

that has held life between its lips
so long,
it seems so long
since life left it wrecked there.

Winter's frosty standstill
will just leave the lips clear
as on a bridge
of would-be sunshine.

But now the intensification
of light in the lower sky
like a stairway outside
the side of a house

acts directly on the blood,
not the mind, to make the sea
appear more light than water,
familiar as a fireside.

The Wake Sofa

If your name did not appear so
on tombs and grocers' shops,
I could rethink your spade-pressed fields
into commonplace, uncultivated land again.
This sealed-up, cloud-darkened country
would not push its leaves into that unroofed
sea-lit room you whipped up without wine.

I have not spoken words with roots
since I saw you;
the light around my eyes
from your transparent grass
is the tightness around everyone's lips.
Though there was all last August
to be spoken to or let go
and the riper air blew shadows bowl-shaped,
it's over, this summer too.

The hedge of daily telephone calls, cut away,
till it was said by the painfully lengthened
garden: the blue and white mosaic,
where your knowing the news
seemed to get bluer, worn down
by the pure lip of the sea
to this perfectly smooth sky,
won't pitchfork me up into living again.

So very capable of dying, walking away
from your hard chair, a pilgrim from your flesh.
Though everyone is wayfaring,
you see ahead of yourself
like a handful of grain flung in a semi-circle,
a feeling that has been existing forever,
but hasn't returned, and isn't enough for you.

In the turn of your book a cloud
formed in my neck and laid my arm
on your shoulder like some twisted necklace.
The sea, as I go out of the door,
laps like a redness over the smoke-grey floor,
a river under a river, underflowing.

Your eyes fall into their own
midday weight: I rub their frail ache in.
You change by what I hear of you
into the dim fluid of a year,
but when tables are crowded with flowers,
and autumn deepens its flame again,
I will be fertilised only by your thinking it:

on a black-grained day,
when women open their cloaks in firelit houses,
scarcely burning, flinging out their fingers,
I shall see what it meant
when I said I dreamt
your bitter sail near morning in my throat.

Black Note Study

Now you are my Northerner,
more first than first love.
Your eyes just show me the smoke
settling on roads open to you
only because they are pure offerings.
All the locks of that country
turn with that key.
Sound travels four times as fast there,
the mouth I have always felt as world
is itself already a fraction
in a family of sounds, a sleep nest
of frozen music, not into the winter.

Such a violent return
to your unfrozen self, it is still possible
to change the names of your addressless
villages. The bone structure
of your picture
has inverted its spinning shape
so it makes sense at any speed.
Like two halves of a nest,
our fingers lie so close together
they almost overlap
or as the body moves within clothing.
Though you have moved your entire hand
to a new starting-point, what I play
with my thumb you are playing
with your fifth finger.

I hear two voices without either
disturbing the other – four harmonies
where there was only one.
One voice spells out the same notes
as the other in reverse order.
One violinist starts at the end,
the other at the beginning,
the backward version fits perfectly
against the forward.

The gap between our hands is no wider
than the middle section of a ship,
which used to be sure of its sun,
or the soundpost joining an instrument
inside, knowing the sky by heart.
And it's nothing to do with proximity
on the keyboard, or the playing length
of the string, on my unaccompanied cello,
if a single chord is repeated over thirty times,
or a note of C- or E-ness
is tied over into that blank space,
held like an undeniable
gull-screech underhand.

The Finder Has Become the Seeker

Sleep easy, supposed fatherhood,
resembling a flowerbed.
Though I extract you here and now
from the soil, open somehow
your newly opened leaves:
I like to breathe what ought to be.

You desire to exist through me;
I want to disappear exhausted in you.
We are things squeezed out, like lips,
not that which serves as coverings –
give me the strength to distinguish myself
from you, such ill-matched wings.

Night furs you, winter clothes you,
Homerically studded in your different planting.
You jangle the keys of the language
you are not using, your understanding
of sunlight is more language than that,
your outcast sounds scatter their fluid carpet.

Your mouth works beyond desolation and glass.
Your mask draws nearer to the other mask.
Your tongue, layered with air, presses a triple breath.
Your thinking fingers possess the acoustic earth:
oh do not heal, dip your travelling eye
the length of my so tightly conceived journey!

Elegy for an Irish Speaker

Numbered day,
night only just beginning,
be born very slowly, stay
with me, impossible to name.

Do I know you, Miss Death,
by your warrant, your heroine's head
pinned against my hero's shoulder?
The seraphim are as cold
to each other in Paradise:
and the room of a dying man
is open to everyone.
The knitting together of your two spines
is another woman
reminding of a wife, his life
surrounds you as a sun,
consumes your light.

Are you waiting to be fertilized,
dynamic death, by his dark company?
To be warmed in your wretched
overnight lodgings
by his kind words and small talk
and powerful movements?
He breaks away from your womb
to talk to me,
he speaks so with my consciousness
and not with words, he's in danger
of becoming a poetess.

Roaming root of multiple meanings,
he shouts himself out
in your narrow amphora,
your tasteless, because immortal, wine.
The instant of recognition
is unsweet to him, scarecrow word
sealed up, second half
of a poetic simile lost somewhere.

119

Most foreign and cherished reader,
I cannot live without
your trans-sense language,
the living furrow of your spoken words
that plough up time.
Instead of the real past
with its deep roots,
I have yesterday,
I have minutes when
you burn up the past
with your raspberry-coloured farewell
that shears the air. Bypassing
everything, even your frozen body,
with your full death, the no-road-back
of your speaking flesh.

The Albert Chain

Like an accomplished terrorist, the fruit hangs
from the end of a dead stem, under a tree
riddled with holes like a sieve. Breath smelling
of cinnamon retires into its dream to die there.
Fresh air blows in, morning breaks, then the mists
close in; a rivulet of burning air
pumps up the cinders from their roots,
but will not straighten in two radiant months
the twisted forest. Warm as a stable,
close to the surface of my mind,
the wild cat lies in the suppleness of life,
half-stripped of its skin, and in the square
beyond, a squirrel stoned to death
has come to rest on a lime tree.

I am going back into war, like a house
I knew when I was young: I am inside,
a thin sunshine, a night within a night,
getting used to the chalk and clay and bats
swarming in the roof. Like a dead man

attached to the soil which covers him,
I have fallen where no judgment can touch me,
its discoloured rubble has swallowed me up.
For ever and ever, I go back into myself:
I was born in little pieces, like specks of dust,
only an eye that looks in all directions can see me.
I am learning my country all over again,
how every inch of soil has been paid for
by the life of a man, the funerals of the poor.

I met someone I believed to be on the side
of the butchers, who said with tears, 'This
is too much.' I saw you nailed to a dry rock,
drawing after you under the earth the blue fringe
of the sea, and you cried out 'Don't move!'
as if you were already damned. You are muzzled
and muted, like a cannon improvised from an iron
pipe. You write to me generally at nightfall,
careful of your hands, bruised against bars:
already, in the prime of life, you belong
to the history of my country, incapable
in this summer of treason, of deliberate treason,
charming death away with the rhythm of your arm.

As if one part of you were coming to the rescue
of the other, across the highest part of the sky,
in your memory of the straight road flying past,
I uncovered your feet as a small refuge,
damp as winter kisses in the street,
or frost-voluptuous cider over
a fire of cuttings from the vine.
Whoever goes near you is isolated
by a double row of candles. I could escape
from any other prison but my own
unjust pursuit of justice
that turns one sort of poetry into another.

Pulsus Paradoxus

At first something like an image was there:
he had for me a pre-love which leaves
everything as it is. We do not see everything
as something, everything that is brown,
we take for granted the incorruptible
colouredness of the colour. But a light
shines on them from behind, they do not
themselves glow. As a word has only
an aroma of meaning, as the really faithful
memory is the part of a wound
that goes quiet.

Keeping magic out has itself the character
of magic – a picture held us captive
and we could not get outside it
for it lay in our language in the uniform
of a force that no longer existed.
Peace was the target he was aiming at,
the point at which doubt becomes senseless,
the last thing that will find a home.

Shelmalier

Looked after only by the four womb-walls,
if anything curved in the ruined city his last hour
it was his human hands, bituminous, while all laws
were aimed at him, returning to the metre of a star:
like a century about to be over, a river trying
to film itself, detaching its voice from itself,
he qualified the air of his own dying,
his brain in folds like the semi-open rose of grief.
His eyes recorded calm and keen this exercise,
deep-seated, promising avenues, they keep their kingdom:
it is I who am only just left in flight, exiled
into an outline of time, I court his speech, not him.
This great estrangement has the destination of a rhyme.
The trees of his heart breathe regular, in my dream.

Blue Doctrine

The boundary of the light will not coincide
with the edge of the window.
With me by his side he is not compelled
to think about me,
nor would he care
whether my lips were more or less red.

I feel like breaking the enchantment
with a fierce shout, rendering needless
the deception of colour, or writing
each sentence in a different colour
so it resembles a little flag,
having for background a half-sun.

For those who sit in the darkened
doorways of their dwellings devoid
of doors, the trouble-adding sound
of bells can mean whatever you want
it to – mobilization, a warlike tempo,
passive defence.

Over my head a bat unfolds it wings
like hands that seem to seek
each other's warmth, or an eyelid
opened in the pulse of a glove,
as in the coat of arms
of my native city.

The air of the first night of summer,
not a moment too early, not a moment
too late, leaps into my paper bed
in the uniform of sleep
from the waist
down.

First a long stretch, then mistakes,
then jumping by tens, until his stomach
is tight against my thighs, ending
in a row of noughts,
as if he had been with a woman.

Plague Song

Torso of music on the crutch of Irish –
this is the netted green in you,
marching and counter-marching,
requiring two separate orchestras.

Already under sentence,
with autumn at your centre as well
as at your edges, the join between
the centuries breaks in a tensed
ecstasy that moves and satisfies.

Shadow makes a fulcrum of its own body
and stretches into more places
than the coinage of the day.

The notes that lay most naturally,
being composed through, for them
the dream may not have been dreamt out,

soundscape of dotted rhythms and heavy
blows, with drums holding the home key,
and a horn that has heard what the violin wanted.

The Jasmine-Picker

Time stopped watching
wherever it comes from
and nowhere touched.

All winter movements
swooped out of their slumber:
the facile hand that braided
the barbed wire forgot
the murmur of roses.

The string of doves
around her neck
swam and breast-fed
at every level of his heart.

His face stayed ineloquent,
rolled up, sowing
a year's worth
of time-bound children.

Their insurgent faces
guarded by slaves
to give the impression
of mastery over a country.

The prayerless non-colour
of the provincial hearses
established their beloved dust
around the ring of death
like a colour squeezed
from a mauve
and willow-green flower.

So, disinvited,
the wrist-pleats' downward swing
soared above the enchantment
of a world trying to live.

125

The Society of the Bomb

The sleep of her lover is her sleep:
it warms her and brings her out to people
like half-making love or the wider now,
exceptionally sunlit spring.

Before violence was actually offered
to us, we followed a trail of words
into the daylight, those palest and clearest
blues, and all the snow to come.

Nuala Ní Dhomhnaill

Póg

Do phóg fear eile mé
i lár mo bheola,
do chuir sé a theanga
istach i mo bhéal.
Nior bhraitheas faic.
Dúrt leis
"Téir abhaile, a dheartháirín,
tán tú ólta
is tá do bhean thall sa doras
ag fanacht."

Ach nuair a chuimhním
ar do phógsa
critheann mo chromáin
is imíonn
a bhfuil eatarthu
ina lacht.

Kiss

Straight on my mouth
another man's kiss.
He put his tongue
between my lips.
I was numb
and said to him
"Little man, go home
you're drunk
your wife waits at the door."

But when I recall
your kiss
I shake, and all
that lies
between my hips
liquifies
to milk.

Translated by Michael Hartnett

Cú Chulainn II

"A mháthair," ol Cú Chulainn,
"raghad chun na macraidhe.
Inis dom cá bhfuilid
is conas a raghad ann.
Táim bréan de bheith ag maireachtaint
ar immealbhoird bhur saolna,
caite i mo chnap ar leac thigh tábhairne
nuair a théann sibh ag ól pórtair,
ag crústadh cloch ar thraenacha
nó ag imirt póiríní le leanaí beaga,
ag féachaint ar na mairt á leagadh
nuair a bhíonn sibh ag búistéireacht
nó ar lasracha na dtinte cnámh
ag léimt sa tsráid go luath Oíche Shin Seáin.

Ach sara bhfágfad
cur uait do chniotáil
is bain an feaig as do bhéal neoimint,
abair liom aon ní amháin
is ná habair níos mó – a leithéid seo,
cé hé m'athair?"
D'fhéach Deichtine, a mháthair,
idir an dá shúil air.
D'oscail sí a béal chun rud a rá
ach dhún aríst é is ní dúirt sí faic.
Ní thugann mná tí stuama
freagra díreach ar cheist chomh dána léi.
Dá ndéanfadh seans go n-imeodh
an domhan mór uile ina raic.

Cú Chulainn II

"Mammy," said Cú Chulainn,
"I will join the grown-ups.
Tell me where they are
and how I'll get to them.
I'm fed up living
on the edges of your lives
thrown in a heap on the pub doorstep
when you go drinking porter,
or tossing stones at passing trains
or marble-playing with kids
seeing the oxen falling
when you are butchering
or seeing the flames of bonfires
on St John's Eve.

But before I leave
put down your knitting
take the fag from your lip a minute
and tell me one thing –
who is my father?"

Deichtine his mother
stared at him
opened her mouth to speak,
closed it again, wordless.
No dedicated housewife would
answer such directness.
If word were said
the whole world would be
in chassis.

Translated by Michael Hartnett

Do Mhelissa

Mo Pháistín Fionn ag rince i gcroí na duimhche,
ribín i do cheann is fáinní óir ar do mhéaranta
duitse nach bhfuil fós ach a cúig nó a sé do bhlianta
tíolacaim gach a bhfuil sa domhan mín mín.

An gearrcach éin ag léimt as tóin na nide
an feileastram ag péacadh sa díog,
an portán glas ag siúl fiarsceabhach go néata,
is leatsa iad le tabhairt faoi ndeara, a iníon.

Bheadh an damh ag súgradh leis an madra allta
an naíonán ag gleáchas leis an nathair nimhe,
luífeadh an leon síos leis an uan caorach
sa domhan úrnua a bhronnfainn ort mín mín.

Bheadh geataí an ghairdín ar leathadh go moch is go déanach,
ní bheadh claimhte lasrach á fhearadh ag Ceiribín,
níor ghá dhuit duilliúr fige mar naprún íochtair
sa domhain úrnua a bhronnfainn ort mín mín.

A iníon bhán, seo dearbhú ó do mháithrín
go mbeirim ar láimh duit an ghealach is an ghrian
is go seasfainn le mo chorp féin idir dhá bhró an mhuilinn
i muilte Dé chun nach meilfí tú mín mín.

Poem For Melissa

My fair-haired child dancing in the dune.
hair be-ribboned, gold rings on your finge.
to you, yet only five or six years old,
I grant you all on this delicate earth.

The fledgeling bird out of the nest
the iris seeding in the drain
the green crab walking neatly sideways:
they are yours to see, my daughter.

The ox would gambol with the wolf
the child would play with the serpent
the lion would lie down with the lamb
in the pasture world I would delicately grant.

Men
Predator

The garden gates forever wide open
no flaming swords in hands of Cherubim
no need for a fig-leaf apron here
in the pristine world I would delicately give.

← a perfect eden ?

Oh white daughter here's your mother's word:
I will put in your hand the sun and the moon
I will stand my body between the millstones
in God's mills so you are not totally ground.

Translated by Michael Hartnett

133

Ceann

Fear is ea Thomas Murphy, fear m'aintín,
a aithníonn ceann thar cheannaibh.
Níl tuama dá n-osclaítear thall i dTeampall Chaitlíona
i bparóiste Fionntrá nach féidir leis gach plaosc ann a rianadh
díreach ach féachaint ar na fiacla. Is nuair a thagann sé
ar chnámh lorgan a briseadh tráth is go bhfuil rian
an chniotála fós le léamh air, tá a fhios aige cé tá aige,
a ainm is a shloinne, is fiú tá cúntas aige ar chonas
a tharla an óspairt.

Ach fós deir sé liom nár thóg sé riamh ina láimh
an rí ar fad orthu, plaosc Thomás a'Chinn.
De Mhuintir Chíobháin ab ea é, anuas ó Chill Uraidh
is bhí sé garbh láidir toirtiúil ina mheon is ina chruth.
Chuaigh sé i ngeall dhá ualach capaill de ribíní feamnaí
le fear ó Rath Fhionáin, mac baintrí,
ach seans buille a bhualadh sa cheann air.
Do bhí mo dhuine go dícheallach ag roghnú a mhaide
is sa deireadh thoigh sé faid ribín úime
ó úim Thomáis Uí Chíobhain. Chuir sé in airde a mhaide
is thug sé slais mhaith láidir timpeall na cluaise air.
Dheim dhá smut den maide is corraí níor dhein Tomás
ach do chuimil sé a chluais is do líon sé a dhá ualach
feamnaí is do bhailibh sé leis abhaile iad.

Anoir ó Átha na Leac ab ea a bhean
is chuaigh sé isteach an chistin chúichi.
Bhí siúinéir an uair sin i gCill Uraidh
is bhí sé ina shuí cois na tine aici.
Bhí cónra déanta aige go cruinn is go beacht
go raibh bileog orlaigh nó orlaigh is ceathrú inti.
'Ba dheas liomsa an fear a chuirfeadh clár isteach
le buille thruip uirthi,' ar seisean.
'Fear gan ainm ná déanfadh é lena cheann,'
arsa Tomás, is do dhruid sé uaidh siar
is do bhuail sé buille bhaitheas glan díreach ar an gcónra
is do chuir sé an clár isteach uirthi.

Ní hionadh mar sin nuair a cuireadh é i bhFionntrá
i dTeampall Chaitlíona go raibh a phlaosc fós le haithint ann.
Ceann Thomás a'Chinn a tugtaí air
is bhíodh daoine ag déanamh iontais do.
Ach dá mhéid é a scrothaíocht ní raibh aon bhreith ag Tomás
    riamh
ar Leanbh Mór an Ghleanna, a chónaigh thiar i nGleann Fán.
Floruit timpeall na bliana 1784, bliain an Droch-Earraigh
deich mbliana nó mar sin roimis bliain Maraithe na bhFear
sa Daingean – níor fhan súgán i gcathaoir nó sop tuí i leaba
nár itheadh an bhliain sin.
Bhí sé sa tairngreacht go dtiocfadh a leithéad ann
is iontas ab ea é. Banlámh anairte a dhéanfadh muinchille
a riosta is an beart bruis a thabharfadh sé anuas ón gcnoc
bhíodh toirt botháin ann. D'aistríodh sé bád
síos is suas is seisear fear fén dtaobh eile dho.
Bhris sé lámh duine lá leis an bhfáscadh a thug sé do.

Tomás Conchúir, is é ag marcaíocht ar a stail bhán
chuaigh sé isteach i dtigh an Linbh mar bhí gaol aige
lena mháthair. Fuair sé muga maide de ghruth is meadhg
is d'ól é go sásta is do shín an muga go dtí an Leanbh.

Níor dhein sé siúd aon ní ach breith ar Thomás Conchúir
is é a bhuladh faoina ascaill is gabháilt amach
an doras leis. Bhí a mháthair ina choinne.
'Ca bhfuileann tú ag dul leis sin?' 'Chun é a chaitheamh
    le haill,'
arsa an Leanbh. Bhí a mháthair ag bladar is ag bladar
is ag tathant is ag fógrú air go dtí sa deireadh
gur scaoil sé leis. Ní raibh an Leanbh an lá sin
ach naoi mbliana d'aois is trí bliana déag a bhí sé
nuair a cailleadh é. B'éigean do mhórsheisear fear
dul faoin gcomhrainn is tá sé ainmnithe riamh ó shin
ar an bhfear is mó a mhair sa dúthaigh riamh.

Ach cén bhaint atá aige seo go léir liomsa
nó caith uait na céapars, a deireann tú.
Tá, go siúlann na daoine seo go léir, go reigleálta

isteach i mo thaibhraithe. Inné roimh lá
bhí fathach mór d'fhear óg, an Leanbh, ní foláir,
trasna an chuain uainn is bhíos-sa agus na leanaí
ag iarraidh é a mhealladh chughainn anall
tré sholas a lasadh, faoi mar a bheadh tóirse gluaisteáin
ann/as, ann/as, ann/as – trí lasadh fada
is trí cinn ghearra arís, ar chuma S.O.S.
Féachaint an dtuigfeadh sé an scéala
is go dtiocfadh sé i leith;
féachaint an bhféadfaimis teangmháil a dhéanamh leis
    ar deireadh.

The Head

My auntie's man, Tom Murphy, has a talent
For identifying skulls.
There's not a head he wouldn't recognise, any time
They'd open up a tomb in Caitlin's graveyard, over there
In Ventry parish. He knows them by their teeth.
And when he comes across a badly-knitted bone, he reads
The jagged line like script. He'll have the name, the surname,
And a story about how it happened
As long as your arm.

But he tells me there's a skull he's never managed yet
To lay his hands on – the real king of them all, the skull
Of Tom the Head. This was one of the Kavanaghs from
    Killdurrihy,
A great big hulk of a body, with a mind to match.
He made a bargain with this character one day,
A widow's son from Rathanane: two horseloads of kelp
For letting him take a belt at his head.
The character deliberates about his choice of weapon, till
At length he lifts this pannier-pin, and gives the Head
An awful crack on the ear. The stick broke in two bits
While Tommy . . . Tommy never turned a hair, but rubbed
    his earlobe

136

Absentmindedly, and set off homewards
With his two loads of manure.

His wife was from back East, from Annaleck.
So he walks into the kitchen one day, and this joiner
And the wife are hob-nobbing by the fire.
There's a great big coffin made of one-inch – no, an inch
And a quarter – deal boards. 'I'd like to see the man,'
The joiner says, 'who could break one of these boards
With one kick of his boot.'
'It would be an awful runt,'
Says Tom, 'who couldn't do it with his head,' and with that
He puts a cracker of a head-butt
Clean through the coffin.

So it's no wonder, when at last they put him under –
In Ventry parish, in St. Caitlin's graveyard –
That the skull achieved a kind of notoriety.
They called it the Head of Tom the Head
And it became a byword in the district.
But for all his incredible bulk he was a shadow
When you put him up against the Big Child of the Glen.
Glen Fahan was his dwelling-place, and in the year of 1784
Or thereabouts, he was at his peak. That was the Year of
    the Bad Spring,
About ten years, come to think of it, before the Massacre
In Dingle. Straw ropes and mattresses were in short supply
That year; the cattle – and the people – had them ate.
It had been prophesied that such a one would come,
And so the legend was born. The makings of the wristband
    of his shirt
Would take a yard of linen, and the brushwood
That he'd gather on the mountain would provide a good-sized
    shed.
Hauling boats, or launching them, the Child would be on
    one side,
Seven strong men on the other.
And he broke this boyo's arm one day, with one twist of his
    wrist.

137

One day Tommy Connor was abroad on his white stallion.
He walks into the Child's place – he was some relation of the
    mother –
Lifts a wooden mug of curds and whey, and knocks it straight
    back.
He hands the Child the empty mug.
What does the Child do?
He oxters Tommy up and heads out the door with him.
The mammy jumps up. 'What in God's name, Child, are
    you at?'
'I'm gonna toss him off the cliff,' the Child says,
And it took the ma to call him all the names of the day
Before he let him go. He was nine at that time; thirteen
When he died. It took six strong men
To lift the coffin, and he's known to this day
As the biggest child that ever roamed these parts.

But what has this to do with anything, you might say, all this
    bullshit?
Just this: these people swim into my ken with marvellous
Regularity. Just yesterday, before first light, an enormous giant
    of a youngster –
It could only be the Child – was signalling across the bay to us,
And the children and myself were trying to guide him over
    to our side,
Flashing a light – a car flashlight, maybe – on/off, on/
Off, on/off . . . three long bursts and three
Short bursts, three long ones again, for all the world like
    S.O.S. –
Hoping he would get the message, trying to see if he would
    talk to us,
Or, finally, if we could talk to him.

Translated by Ciaran Carson

Féar Suaithinseach

Nuair a bhís i do shagart naofa
i lár an Aifrinn, faoi do róbaí corcra
t'fhallaing lín, do stól, do chasal,
do chonnaicis m'aghaidhse ins an slua
a bhí ag teacht chun comaoineach chughat
is thit uait an abhlainn bheannaithe.

Mise, ní dúrt aon ní ina thaobh.
Bhí náire orm.
Bhí glas ar mo bhéal.
Ach fós do luigh sé ar mo chroí
mar dhealg láibe, gur dhein sé slí
dó fhéin istigh im ae is im lár
gur dhóbair go bhfaighinn bás dá bharr.

Ní fada nó gur thiteas 'on leabaidh;
oideasaí leighis do triaileadh ina gcéadtaibh,
do tháinig chugham dochtúirí, sagairt is bráithre
is n'fhéadadar mé a thabhairt chun sláinte
ach thugadar suas i seilbh bháis mé.

Is téigí amach, a fheara,
tugaíg libh rámhainn is speala
corráin, grafáin is sluaiste.
Réabaíg an seanafhothrach,
bearraíg na sceacha, glanaíg an luifearnach,
an slámas fáis, an brus, an ainnise
a fhás ar thalamh bán mo thubaiste.

Is ins an ionad inar thit
an chomaoine naofa féach go mbeidh
i lár an bhiorlamais istigh
toirtín d'fhéar suaithinseach.

Tagadh an sagart is lena mhéireanna
beireadh sé go haiclí ar an gcomaoine naofa
is tugtar chugham í, ar mo theanga
leáfaidh sí, is éireod aniar sa leaba
chomh slán folláin is a bhíos is mé i mo leanbh.

Miraculous Grass

There you were in your purple vestments
half-way through the Mass, an ordained priest
under your linen alb and chasuble and stole:
and when you saw my face in the crowd
for Holy Communion
the consecrated host fell from your fingers.

I felt shame, I never
mentioned it once,
my lips were sealed.
But still it lurked in my heart
like a thorn under mud, and it
worked itself in so deep and sheer
it nearly killed me.

Next thing then, I was laid up in bed.
Consultants came in their hundreds,
doctors and brothers and priests,
but I baffled them all: I was
incurable, they left me for dead.

So out you go, men,
out with the spades and scythes,
the hooks and shovels and hoes.
Tackle the rubble,
cut back the bushes, clear off the rubbish,
the sappy growth, the whole straggle and mess
that infests my green unfortunate field.

And there where the sacred wafer fell
you will discover
in the middle of the shooting weeds
a clump of miraculous grass.

The priest will have to come then
with his delicate fingers, and lift the host
and bring it to me and put it on my tongue.

Where it will melt, and I will rise in the bed
as fit and well as the youngster I used to be.

Translated by Seamus Heaney

An Crann

Do tháinig bean an leasa
le Black & Decker,
do ghearr sí anuas mo chrann.
D'fhanas im óinseach ag féachaint uirthi
faid a bhearraigh sí na brainsí
ceann ar cheann.

Tháinig m'fhear céile abhaile tráthnóna.
Chonaic sé an crann.
Bhí an gomh dearg air,
ní nach ionadh. Dúirt sé
'Canathaobh nár stopais í?
Nó cad is dóigh léi?
Cad a cheapfadh sí
dá bhfaighinnse Black & Decker
is dul chun a tí
agus crann ansúd a bhaineas léi,
a ghearradh anuas sa ghairdín?'

Tháinig bean an leasa thar n-ais ar maidin.
Bhíos fós ag ithe mo bhricfeasta.
D'iarr sí orm cad dúirt m'fhear céile.
Dúrsta léi cad dúirt sé,
go ndúirt sé cad is dóigh léi,
is cad a cheapfadh sí
dá bhfaigheadh sé siúd Black & Decker
is dul chun a tí
is crann ansúd a bhaineas léi
a ghearradh anuas sa ghairdín.

'Ó,' ar sise, *'that's very interesting.'*
Bhí béim ar an *very*
Bhí cling leis an *–ing.*
Do labhair sí ana-chiúin.

Bhuel, b'shin mo lá-sa,
pé ar bith sa tsaol é,
iontaithe bunoscionn.
Thit an tóin as mo bholg
is faoi mar a gheobhainn lascadh cic
nó leacadar sna baotháin
líon taom anbhainne isteach orm
a dhein chomh lag san mé
gurb ar éigin a bhí ardú na méire ionam
as san go ceann trí lá.

Murab ionann is an crann
a dh'fhan ann, slán.

As for the Quince

There came this bright young thing
with a Black & Decker
and cut down my quince-tree.
I stood with my mouth hanging open
while one by one
she trimmed off the branches.

When my husband got home that evening
and saw what had happened
he lost the rag,
as you might imagine.
'Why didn't you stop her?
What would she think
if I took the Black & Decker
round to her place

and cut down a quince-tree
belonging to her?
What would she make of that?'

Her ladyship came back next morning
while I was at breakfast.
She enquired about his reaction.
I told her straight
that he was wondering how she'd feel
if he took a Black & Decker
round to her house
and cut down a quince-tree of hers,
 et cetera et cetera.

'O,' says she, 'that's very interesting.'
There was a stress on the 'very'.
She lingered over the 'ing'.
She was remarkably calm and collected.

These are the times that are in it, so,
all a bit topsy-turvy.
The bottom falling out of my belly
as if I had got a kick up the arse
or a punch in the kidneys.
A fainting-fit coming over me
that took the legs from under me
and left me so zonked
I could barely lift a finger
till Wednesday.

As for the quince, it was safe and sound
and still somehow holding its ground.

Translated by Paul Muldoon

Chomh Leochaileach le Sliogán

Chomh leochaileach le sliogán
a caitheadh suas ar chladach
seasaim lasmuigh ded dhoras
san iarnóin.
Clingeann an clog i bhfad istigh
go neamheaglach
is baineann macalla as na seomraí folamha
im chomhair.

Istigh sa chistin tá raidió
ag stealladh popcheoil
is músclaíonn spré bheag dóchais
istigh im bhráid
ach nuair a chuimhním arís air
is cleas é seo i gcoinne robálaithe
agus is fada fuar folamh an feitheamh agam
gan troist do choiscéime ar an bhfód.

Clingim arís
is éiríonn fuaim mhacallach
trés na seomraí arda,
suas an staighre cláir.
Aithním trí pholl na litreach
ar na toisí Seoirseacha
struchtúr laitíse an chriostail
a cheileann nó a nochtann Dia.

Tá rós dearg i gcróca
ar bhord sa halla.
Tá geansaí ag crochadh
leis an mbalastráid.
Tá litreacha oscailte ina luí timpeall
ar an urlár go neafaiseach
i mball ar bith
níl blas ná rian duit le fáil.

Istigh sa seomra suite
ar an gclabhar
tá cárta poist a tháinig chughat aniar
ód ghrá geal. Maíonn sí
gurb é seo an chéad phost nó litir
a gheobhair id thigh nua.
Is air tá radharc gnáthúil turasóireachta
de Bhrú na Bóinne.

Tagairt é seo a thuigeann tú
gan amhras
don *hieros gamos*
an pósadh a deineadh ar Neamh.
Is lasmuigh de chiorcal
teolaí bhur lánúnachais
tá fuar agam fanacht sa doras
i mo dhílleachtaí, i mo spreas.

Tá oighear á shéideadh
trí phóirsí fada gaofara
sa phaibhiliún
is íochtaraí i mo lár.
Tá na seolphíobáin mhothála
reoite ina stangadh.
Tá tonnbhualadh mo chroí
mar fharraigí aduaine.

Is mo léan mo cheann mailéid,
mo chloigeann peirce,
os comhair an dorias iata seo
cad leis a bhfuil mo shúil?
Nuair a chlingeann an clog
ar chuma an Aingil Mhuire
ab ann a cheapaim go n-osclóidh na Flaithis
is go dtuirlingeoidh orm colur?

Mar is istigh sa sícé amháin
a tharlíonn míorúiltí
an cheana, an mhaithiúnachais

is an ghrá
mar is i dtaibhrithe amháin
a bhíonn an ghrian is an ré ag soilsiú
le chéile is spéir na maidne
orthu araon ag láú.

As Fragile as a Shell

As fragile as a shell
cast up on a rocky shore,
I stand outside your door
in the afternoon. The bell
rings deep in the house,
echoing in the long, empty rooms.

The kitchen radio howls
rock music and, for a moment,
I feel a surge of hope; but then
I realize it is only there
to deter thieves
and a long wait lies before me
with no sound of your step.

I ring again, and the echo rises
among high ceilings, wooden stairs.
Peering through the letter-box
I recognize in the Georgian proportions
an intricate crystal-like structure
which bodies forth and hides a god.

A red rose stands in a vase
on the hall table; a sweater
hangs from the banister.
Unopened letters lie about
carelessly on the floor;
but nowhere is there a sign
of you to be seen.

On the drawing-room mantelpiece
a postcard from your lover
boasts that hers is the first
mail in your new house; it shows
a simple tourist view
of the tumulus at Newgrange.

There is a reference
 – not lost on you, of course –
to the *hieros gamos*, the marriage
made in heaven. Outside
the warm conspiracy of your love
I stand, a nobody,
an orphan at the door.

An icy wind blows through the cold porches
of the farthest pavilions
in the depths of my soul;
the rivers of emotion are frozen solid,
my heart beats wildly
like strange and treacherous seas.

Damn my wooden head, my feather brain,
why am I waiting here
at your closed door?
When the bell peals inside
like the Angelus, do I really
expect the sky to open
and a dove
to descend upon me from above?

It is only in the soul
that the miracles take place
of love, forgiveness and grace;
it is only in dreams
that the sun and moon shine together
in a bright sky
while day dawns on them both.

Translated by Derek Mahon

Gan do Chuid Éadaigh

Is fearr liom tú
gan do chuid éadaigh ort,
do léine shíoda
is do charabhat,
do scáth fearthainne foi t'ascaill
is do chulaith
trí phíosa faiseanta
le barr feabhais táilliúrachta,

do bhróga ar a mbíonn
i gcónaí snas,
do lámhainní craiceann eilite
ar do bhois,
do hata *crombie*
feircthe ar fhaobhar na cluaise –
ní chuireann siad aon ruainne
le do thuairisc,

mar thíos fúthu
i ngan fhios don slua
tá corp gan mhaisle, mháchail
nó míbhua
lúfaireacht ainmhí allta,
cat mór a bhíonn amuigh
san oíche
is a fhágann sceimhle ina mharbhshruth.

Do ghuailne leathan fairsing
is do thaobh
chomh slim le sneachta séidte
ar an sliabh;
do dhrom, do bhásta singil
is i do ghabhal
an rúta
go bhfuil barr pléisiúrtha ann.

Do chraiceann atá chomh dorcha
is slim
le síoda go mbeadh tiús veilbhite
ina shníomh
is é ar chumhracht airgid luachra
nó meadhg na habhann
go ndeirtear faoi
go bhfuil suathadh fear is ban ann.

Mar sin is dá bhrí sin
is tú ag rince liom anocht
cé go mb'fhearr liom tú
gan do chuid éadaigh ort,
b'fhéidir nárbh aon díobháil duit
gléasadh anois ar an dtoirt
in ionad leath ban Éireann
a mhilleadh is a lot.

rt
ner see you nude –

                under your oxter
in case   iny day,
the three-piece seersucker
suit that's so incredibly trendy,

your snazzy loafers
and, la-di-da,
a pair of gloves
made from the skin of a doe,

then, to top it all, a crombie hat
set at a rak-
ish angle – none of these add
up to more than the icing on the cake.

For, unbeknownst to the rest
of the world, behind the outward
show lies a body unsurpassed
for beauty, without so much as a wart

or blemish, but the brill-
iant slink of a wild animal, a dream-
cat, say, on the prowl,
leaving murder and mayhem

in its wake. Your broad, sinewy
shoulders and your flank
smooth as the snow
on a snow-bank.

Your back, your slender waist,
and, of course,

150

the root that is the very seat
of pleasure, the pleasure-source.

Your skin so dark, my beloved,
and soft
as silk with a hint of velvet
in its weft,

smelling as it does of meadowsweet
or 'watermead'
that has the power, or so it's said,
to drive men and women mad.

For that reason alone, if for no other,
when you come with me to the dance tonight
(though, as you know, I'd much prefer
to see you nude)

it would probably be best
for you to pull on your pants and vest
rather than send
half the women of Ireland totally round the bend.

Translated by Paul Muldoon

Cailleach

Taibhríodh dom gur mé an talamh,
gur mé paróiste Fionntrá
ar a fhaid is ar a leithead,
soir, siar, faoi mar a shíneann sí.
Gurbh é grua na Maoilinne grua
mo chinn agus Sliabh an Iolair
mo chliathán aniar;
gurbh iad leaca na gcnoc
mo loirgne is slat
mo dhroma is go raibh an fharraige
ag líric mo dhá throigh
ag dhá charraig sin na Páirce,
Rinn Dá Bhárc na Fiannaíochta.

Bhí an taibhreamh chomh beo
nuair a dhúisíos ar maidin
gur fhéachas síos féachaint an raibh,
de sheans, mo dhá chois fliuch.
Ansan d'imíos is dhearmhadas
a raibh tarlaithe, ó,
tá dhá bliain is breis
anois ann, déarfainn
go dtí le fíordhéanaí
gur cuireadh i gcuimhne arís dom
fuíoll mo thromluí
de bharr líonrith m'iníne.

Bhíomair thíos ar an dtráigh
is bhí sí traochta.
Do chas sí abhaile
ach do leanas-sa orm ag siúl romham.
Ní fada gur chuala í
ag teacht chugham agus saothar uirthi,
í ag pusaíl ghoil le teann coisíochta.
'Cad tá, ort?' 'Ó a Mhaim, táim sceimhlithe.
Tuigeadh dom go raibh na cnoic ag bogadaíl,
gur fathach mná a bhí ag luascadh a cíocha,
is go n-éireodh sí aniar agus mise d'íosfadh.'

Hag

Once I dreamt I was the earth,
the parish of Ventry its length and breadth,
east and west, as far as it runs,
that the brow of the Maoileann
was my forehead, Mount Eagle
the swell of my flank,
the side of the mountain
my shanks and backbone,
that the sea was lapping
the twin rocks of my feet,
the twin rocks of Parkmore
from the old Fenian tales.

That dream was so real
that when I woke next morning
I glanced down to see if, perchance,
my feet were still wet.
Then off I went, and promptly forgot
all about my vision until,
O, when was it exactly, nearly
two years later, the fright
of my daughter stirred again
the dregs of that dream.

We were strolling the strand
but she was so dead-beat
she turned towards home, while
I trudged onwards alone.
Before I got far, I heard
her come running back, snivelling
and sobbing at every step's breath.
'What's wrong?' 'O, Mam, I'm scared stiff,
I thought I saw the mountains heaving
like a giantess, with her breasts swaying,
about to loom over, and gobble me up.'

Translated by John Montague

153

Ceist na Teangan

Cuirim mo dhóchas ar snámh
i mbáidín teangan
faoi mar a leagfá naíonán
i gcliabhán
a bheadh fite fuaite
de dhuilleoga feileastraim
is bitiúmin agus pic
bheith cuimilte lena thóin

ansan é a leagadh síos
i measc na ngiolcach
is coigeal na mban sí
le taobh na habhann,
féachaint n'fheadaraís
cá dtabharfaidh an sruth é,
féachaint, dála Mhaoise,
an bhfóirfidh iníon Fharoinn?

The Language Issue

I place my hope on the water
in this little boat
of the language, the way a body might put
an infant

in a basket of intertwined
iris leaves,
its underside proofed
with bitumen and pitch,

then set the whole thing down amidst
the sedge
and bulrushes by the edge
of a river

154

only to have it borne hither and thither,
not knowing where it might end up;
in the lap, perhaps,
of some Pharaoh's daughter.

Translated by Paul Muldoon

Feis

1

Nuair a éiríonn tú ar maidin
is steallann ionam
seinneann ceolta sí na cruinne
istigh im chloigeann.
Taistealaíonn an ga gréine
caol is lom
síos an pasáiste dorcha
is tríd an bpoll

sa bhfardoras
is ri22ann solas ribe
ar an urlár cré
sa seomra iata
is íochtaraí go léir.
Atann ansan is téann i méid
is i méid go dtí go líontar
le solas órga an t-aireagal go léir.

Feasta
beidh na hoícheanta níos giorra.
Raghaidh achar gach lae i bhfaid is i bhfaid.

2

Nuair a osclaím mo shúile
ag teacht aníos chun aeir
tá an spéir
gorm.
Canann éinín aonair
ar chrann.

155

Is cé bhfuil an teannas
briste
is an ghlaise
ídithe ón uain
is leacht meala leata
mar thúis
ar fuaid an domhain,
fós le méid an tochta
atá eadrainn
ní labhrann ceachtar againn
oiread is focal
go ceann tamaill mhaith.

3
Dá mba dhéithe sinn
anseo ag Brú na Bóinne –
tusa Sualtamh nó an Daghdha,
mise an abhainn ghlórmhar –

do stadfadh an ghrian is an ré
sa spéir ar feadh bliana is lae
ag cur buaine leis an bpléisiúr
atá eadrainn araon.

Faraoir, is fada ó dhéithe
sinne, créatúirí nochta.
Ní stadann na ranna neimhe
ach ar feadh aon nóiméad neamhshíoraí amháin.

4
Osclaíonn rós istigh im chroí.
Labhrann cuach im bhéal.
Léimeann gearrcach ó mo nead.
Tá tóithín ag macnas i ndoimhneas mo mhachnaimh.

5

Cóirím an leaba
i do choinne, a dhuine
nach n-aithním
thar m'fhear céile.

Tá nóiníní leata
ar an bpilliúr is ar an adharta.
Tá sméara dubha
fuaite ar an mbraillín.

6

Leagaim síos trí bhrat id fhianaise:
brat deora,
brat allais,
brat fola.

7

Mo scian trím chroí tú.
Mo sceach trím ladhar tú.
Mo cháithnín faoi m'fhiacail.

8

Thaibhrís dom arís aréir:
bhíomair ag siúl láimh ar láimh amuigh faoin spéir.
Go hobann do léimis os mo chomhair
is bhain greim seirce as mo bhráid.

9

Bhíos feadh na hoíche
ag tiomáint síos bóithre do thíre
i gcarr spóirt béaloscailte
is gan tú faram.
Ghaibheas thar do thigh
is bhí do bhean istigh
sa chistin.
Aithním an sáipéal
ag a n-adhrann tú.

10

Smid thar mo bhéal ní chloisfir,
mo theanga imithe ag an gcat.
Labhrann mo lámha dhom.
Caipín snámha iad faoi bhun do chloiginn
dod chosaint ar oighear na bhfeachtaí bhfliuch.
Peidlhleacáin iad ag tóraíocht beatha
ag eitealaigh that mhóinéar do choirp.

11

Nuair a dh'fhágas tú
ar an gcé anocht
d'oscail trinse ábhalmhór
istigh im ucht
chomh doimhin sin
ná líonfar
fiú dá ndáilfí
as aon tsoitheach
Sruth na Maoile, Muir Éireann
agus Muir nIocht.

Carnival

1

When you rise in the morning
and pour into me
an unearthly music
rings in my ears.
A ray of sunshine comes
slender and spare
down the dark passageway
and through the gap

in the lintel
to trace a light-scroll
on the mud floor
in the nethermost
sealed chamber.
Then it swells
and swells until a golden glow
fills the entire oratory.

From now on
the nights will be getting shorter
and the days longer and longer.

2

When I open my eyes
to come up for air
the sky
is blue.
A single bird sings
in a tree.
And though the tension
is released
and the chill
gone from the air
and a honeyed breath spreads
like frankincense
about the earth

such is the depth of emotion
we share
that neither of us speaks
as much as a word
for ages and ages.

    3
If we were gods
here at Newgrange –
you Sualtam or the Daghda,
myself the famous river –

we could freeze the sun
and the moon
for a year and a day
to perpetuate the pleasure
we have together.

Alas, it's far from gods
we are, but bare, forked creatures.
The heavenly bodies stop
only for a single, transitory moment.

    4
A rose opens in my heart.
A cuckoo sings in my throat.
A fledgeling leaps from my nest.
A dolphin plunges through my deepest thoughts.

    5
I straighten the bed
for you, sweetheart:
I cannot tell
you and my husband apart.

There are daisies strewn
on the pillow and bolster:
the sheets are embroidered
with blackberry-clusters.

6

I lay down three robes before you:
a mantle of tears,
a coat of sweat,
a gown of blood,

7

You are a knife through my heart.
You are a briar in my fist.
You are a bit of grit between my teeth.

8

I dreamt of you again last night:
we were walking hand in hand through the countryside
when you suddenly ambushed
me and gave me a lovebite on my chest.

9

I spent all last night
driving down the byroads of your parish
in an open sports car
without you near me.
I went past your house
and glimpsed your wife
in the kitchen.
I recognise the chapel
at which you worship.

10

You won't hear a cheep from me.
The cat has got my tongue.
My hands do all the talking.
They're a swimming cap about your head
to protect you from the icy currents.
They're butterflies searching for sustenance
over your body's meadow.

11

When I left you
at the quay tonight
an enormous trench opened up
in my core
so profound
it would not be filled
even if you were to pour
from one utensil
the streams of the Mull of Kintyre
and the Irish Sea and the English Channel.

Translated by Paul Muldoon

An Bhatráil

Thugas mo leanbhán liom aréir ón lios
ar éigean.
Bhí sé lán suas de mhíola is de chnathacha
is a chraiceann chomh smiotaithe is chomh gargraithe
go bhfuilim ó mhaidin ag cur ceiríní teo lena thóin
is ag cuimilt *Sudocrem* dá chabhail
ó bhonn a choise go clár a éadain.

Trí bhanaltra a bhí aige ann
is deoch bhainne tugtha ag beirt acu dó.
Dá mbeadh an tríú duine acu tar éis tál air
bheadh deireadh go deo agam leis.
Bhíodar á chaitheamh go neamheaglach
ó dhuine go chéile,
á chur ó láimh go láimh, ag rá
'Seo mo leanbhsa, chughat do leanbhsa.
Seo mo leanbhsa, chughat do leanbhsa.'

Thángas eatarthu isteach de gheit
is ruas ar chiotóg air.
Thairrigíos trí huaire é tré urla an tsnáith ghlais
a bhí i mo phóca agam.

Nuair a tháinig an fear caol dubh romham
ag doras an leasa
dúrt leis an áit a fhágaint láithreach
nó go sáfainn é.
Thugas faobhar na scine coise duibhe
don sceach a bhí sa tslí
romham is a dhá cheann i dtalamh aige.

Bhuel, tá san go maith is níl go holc.
Tá fíor na croise bainte agam
as tlú na tine
is é buailte trasna an chliabháin agam.
Is má chuireann siad aon rud eile nach liom
isteach ann
an diabhal ná gurb é an chaor dhearg
a gheobhaidh sé!
Chaithfinn é a chur i ngort ansan.
Níl aon seans riamh go bhféadfainn dul in aon ghaobhar
d'aon ospidéal leis.
Mar atá
beidh mo leordhóthain dalladh agam
ag iarraidh a chur in iúl dóibh
nach mise a thug an bhatráil dheireanach seo dó.

The Battering

I only just made it home last night with my child
from the fairy fort.
He was crawling with lice and jiggers
and his skin was so red and raw
I've spent all day putting hot poultices on his bottom
and salving him with *Sudocrem*
from stem to stern.

Of the three wet-nurses back in the fort,
two had already suckled him:
had he taken so much as a sip from the third
that's the last I'd have seen of him.

As it was, they were passing him around
with such recklessness,
one to the next, intoning,
'Little laddie to me, to you little laddie.
Laddie to me, la di da, to you laddie.'

I came amongst them all of a sudden
and caught him by his left arm.
Three times I drew him through the lank of undyed wool
I'd been carrying in my pocket.
When a tall, dark stranger barred my way
at the door of the fort
I told him to get off-side fast
or I'd run him through.
The next obstacle was a briar,
both ends of which were planted in the ground:
I cut it with my trusty black-handled knife.

So far, so good.
I've made the sign of the cross
with the tongs
and laid them on the cradle.
If they try to sneak anything past
that's not my own, if they try to pull another fast
one on me, it won't stand a snowball's
chance in hell:
I'd have to bury it out the field.
There's no way I could take it anywhere next
or near the hospital.
As things stand,
I'll have more than enough trouble
trying to convince them that it wasn't me
who gave my little laddie this last battering.

Translated by Paul Muldoon

Lá Chéad Chomaoineach

Ar ndóigh táimid déanach, Sleamhnaímid isteach sa phiú
    deireanach
i mbun an tsáipéil, an cailín beag sa ghúna bán ar an ngrua.
Tá an t-iomann iontrála thart is daoine ag rá an ghnímh aithrí:
A Thiarna déan trócaire, éist le mo ghuí is ná stop do chluais.

Sliochtanna as an mBiobla, an Chré is an Phaidir Eocaraisteach,
gaibheann sias trím chroí ar eiteoga, mar ghlór toirní i stoirm.
Tá an cór ag canadh 'Hosana ins na hardaibh',
gur ag Críost an síol, is ina iothlann go dtugtar sinn.

Is tá an mórshiúl Comaoineach de gharsúin is de ghearrchailí
    beaga
ina ngúnaí cadáis nó a gcultacha le rosette is bonn
ar chuma ealta mhín mhacánta d'eanlaithe feirme
á seoladh faoin bhfásach gan tréadaí ná aoire ina mbun.

Agus is mise an bhean go dubhach ag áireamh a cuid géanna
    sa mbealach,
ag gol is ag gárthaíl, ag lógóireacht don méid a théann ar fán,
iad á stracadh ó chéile ag sionnaigh is mic tíre ár linne-an
    tsaint,
druganna, ailse, gnáthghníomhartha fill is timpistí gluaisteán.

Deinim seó bóthair dínn. Tarrac beag mear ar mo sciorta.
'A Mhaimí, a Mhaimí, canathaobh go bhfuileann tú ag gol?'
Insím deargéitheach: 'Toisc go bhfuil mo chroí ag pléascadh
le teann bróid is mórtais ar lá do chomaoineach, a chuid,'

mar ag féachaint ar an ealta bhán de chailíni beaga,
gach duine acu ina coinnleoir óir ar bhord na banríona,
conas a inseod di i dtaobh an tsaoil atá roimpi,
i dtaobh na doircheachta go gcaithfidh sí siúl tríd

ina haonar, de mo dheargainneoin, is le mo neamhthoil?

First Communion

Fashionably late, as usual, we slide into the last pew,
my daughter in her white communion dress.
The entrance hymn is over. They're half-way through
their 'Hear our prayers, O Lord, have mercy on us.'

The Epistle and Gospel, the Creed, the Eucharist
are thunder-claps going clean
through my heart. 'Hosanna in the highest,'
the choir sings, it is Christ's to sow, to reap, to glean.

The Communion procession of little men
and women in cotton frocks or suits with rosettes and medals
look for all the world like a flock of hens
left to fend for themselves in the middle

of nowhere: I myself am the woman in the road who vexes
over her gaggle of geese, over all those slashed
and burned by our latter-day foxes
and wolves – greed, drugs, cancer, skulduggery, the car-crash.

I make a holy show of us. There's a little tug at my skirt:
'Mammy, why are you moaning?'
'Because,' I bite my tongue, 'because my heart
is filled with pride and joy on the day of your First
    Communion.'

When I look at the little white girl-host
comelier than golden candlesticks at Mother Mary's feet
what can I tell her of the vast
void

through which she must wander alone, over my dead body?

Translated by Paul Muldoon

166

Dípfríos

Cornucopia na haoise, an cóifrín draíochta
as a dtógaimid nua gacha bia agus sean gacha dí –
oiread sólaistí agus d'iarrfadh do bhéal
is gan aon dá ghreim acu ar aon bhlaiseadh.

Bolg soláthair gach teaghlaigh, tobar slánaithe
ár n-ocrais oidhreachtúil na méadaíonn
is ná téann i ndísc. Adhraimid a chairn
ollmhaitheasa. Níl aon teora lena shlaodaibh oigheartha

de mhil is uachtar, de phéitseoga is úlla,
de strúisíní Gaelacha, sceallóga,
ceathrúna mairteola ina fheoil mhionaithe,
iarphroinnte, cístí milse, dhá chaora.

Tá cúig bhollóg aráin ann is dhá iasc
faoi choinne sluate comharsan (má thagann siad).
Is cé chuir an cat marbh seo i measc an spionáiste?
– A Jimín Mháire Thaidhg, gearánfad tú led Mham!

Suite go buacach i gcroílár gach cisteanach
feidhmíonn mar mheafar bunaidh ár sibhialtachta.
Is iad ceolta sí na cruinne seo a chluinimid
ná a mhiam sástachta, cáithníní áthais srutha leictrise.

Momento mori, par excellence, má feaca
riamh ceann, samhlaoid uafar ar an díog
dar di sinn is gur chuici atáimid;
íomhánna greanta gach a gcúblálaimid inti:

marbh agus cruaidh is chomh fuar leis an uaigh.

Deep-Freeze

A modern Horn of Plenty, a magic coffer
from which we take the best of food and drink –
every comestible we might savour
and no two tasting the same. A trunk

of household odds and ends, a healing well
that staves off our deepest hungers, it ne'er o'erbrims
nor gangs dry. We adore its monumental
wealth, its illimitable, icy streams

of milk and honey, apples and peaches,
Irish stews, crinkle-cut chips,
pre-ground legs of beef, batches
of dessert, sweet cakes, a couple of whole sheep.

Here are the five loaves and two Spanish
mackerel to feed the multitude, if ever they come –
Who put the dead cat in with the spinach? –
Jimín Mháire Thadhg! Wait till I tell your mum!

In the dead centre of every kitchen
it holds its own, it glumly stands its ground:
these are the strains of no Otherworldly musicians
but the hum of its alternating current.

From here, if ever I saw one, is a fit
emblem of the ditch or long barrow
from which we derive and wherein lies our fate:
it chills me to the marrow

that we should most truly find ourselves
among its fatted and its golden calves.

Translated by Paul Muldoon

Caitlín

Ní fhéadfa í a thabhairt in aon áit leat,
do thabharfadh sí náire is aithis duit.
Díreach toisc go raibh sí an-mhór ina *vamp*
thiar ins na fichidí, is gur dhamhas sí an Searlastan
le tonntracha méiríneacha ina gruaig dhualach thrilseánach;
gur phabhsae gléigeal í thiar i naoi déag sé déag,
go bhfachthas fornocht i gConnachta í, mar áille na háille,
is ag taisteal bhóithre na Mumhan, mar ghile na gile;
go raibh sí beo bocht, gan locht,
a píob mar an eala, ag teacht taobh leis an dtoinn
is a héadan mar shneachta,

ní théann aon stad uirthi ach ag maíomh
as na seanlaethanta, nuair a bhíodh sí ag ionsaí
na dúthaí is an drúcht ar a bróga,
maidin Domhnaigh is í ag dul go hEochaill
nó ar an mbóthar cothrom idir Corcaigh agus Dúghlas,
Na rudaí iontacha a dúirt an Paorach fúithi
is é mar mhaor ar an loing. Is dúirt daoine eile
go mbeadh an Éirne ina tuilte tréana, is go réabfaí
cnoic. Murab ionann is anois nuair atá sí ina baintreach tréith
go raibh sí an tráth san ina maighdean mhómhar, chaoin,
　　shéimh
is díreach a dóthain céille aici chun fanacht i gcónaí
ar an dtaobh thall den dteorainn ina mbítear de shíor.

Ba dhóigh leat le héisteacht léi nár chuala
sí riamh gur binn béal ina thost, is nach mbíonn
in aon ní ach seal, go gcríonnann an tslat le haois
is fiú dá mba dhóigh le gach spreasán an uair úd
go mba leannán aige féin í, go bhfuil na laethanta san thart.
Cuirfidh mé geall síos leat nár chuala sí leis
mar tá sé de mhórbhua aici agus de dheis
gan aon ní a chloisint ach an rud a 'riúnaíonn í féin.
Tá mil ar an ógbhean aici, dar léi, agus rós breá
ina héadan. Is í sampla í is fearr ar m'aithne
de bhodhaire Uí Laoghaire.

Cathleen

You can't take her out for a night on the town
without her either showing you up or badly letting you down:
just because she made the Twenties roar
with her Black and Tan Bottom – O Terpsichore –
and her hair in a permanent wave;
just because she was a lily grave
in nineteen sixteen; just because she once was spotted
quite naked in Cannought, of beauties most beautied,
or tramping the roads of Moonstare, brightest of the bright;
just because she was poor, without blemish or blight,
high-stepping it by the ocean with her famous swan's prow
and a fresh fall of snow on her broadest of broad brows –

because of all that she never stops bending your ear
about the good old days of yore
when she crept through the country in her dewy high heels
of a Sunday morning, say, on the road to Youghal
or that level stretch between Cork and Douglas.
There was your man Power's ridiculous
suggestion when he was the ship's captain, not to speak
of the Erne running red with abundance and mountain-peaks
laid low. She who is now a widowed old woman
was a modest maiden, meek and mild, but with enough
     gumption
at least to keep to her own
side of the ghostly demarcation, the eternal buffer-zone.

For you'd think to listen to her she'd never heard
that discretion is the better part, that our names are writ
in water, that the greenest stick will wizen:
even if every slubberdegullion once had a dream-vision
in which she appeared as his own true lover,
those days are just as truly over.
And I bet Old Gummy Granny
has taken none of this on board because of her uncanny
knack of hearing only what confirms
her own sense of herself, her honey-nubile form

170

and the red rose, proud rose or canker
tucked behind her ear, in the head-band of her blinkers.

Translated by Paul Muldoon

Tusa

Is tusa, pé thú féin,
an firéan
a thabharfadh cluais le héisteacht,
b'fhéidir, do bhean inste scéil
a thug na cos leí, ar éigean,
ó láthair an chatha.

Níor thugamair féin an samhradh linn
ná an geimhreadh.
Níor thriallamair ar bord loinge
go Meiriceá ná ag lorg ár bhfortúin
le chéile i sli ar bith
ins na tíortha teo thar lear.

Níor ghaibheamair de bharr na gcnoc
ar chapall láidir álainn dubh.
Níor luiomair faoi chrann caorthainn
is an oíche ag cur cuisne.
Ní lu ná mar bhí tinte cnámh
is an adharc á séideadh ar thaobh na gréine.

Eadrainn bhí an fharraige mhór
atá brónach. Eadrainn
bhí na cnoic is na sléibhte
ná casann ar a chéile.

You Are

Whoever you are, you are
The real thing, the witness
Who might lend an ear
To a woman with a story
Barely escaped with her life
From the place of battle.

Spring the sweet spring was not sweet for us
Nor winter neither
We never stepped aboard a ship together
Bound for America to seek
Our fortune, we never
Shared those hot foreign lands.

We did not fly over the high hills
Riding the fine black stallion,
Or lie under the hazel branches
As the night froze about us,
No more than we lit bonfires of celebration
Or blew the horn on the mountainside.

Between us welled the ocean
Waves of grief. Between us
The mountains were forbidding
And the roads long, with no turning.

Translated by Eiléan Ní Chuilleanáin

An tEach Uisce

Ar dtiúis ba ina cuid taibhrí amháin
a thagadh sé chun luí léi.

Ansan lá
go raibh sí in ainm is a bheith ag aoireacht ba
i gCuaisín na gCaorach, (bhí sí ag léamh
The Old Curiosity Shop le Charles Dickens
is gan aon chuimhneamh aici ar bha ná a leithéid)
cad a chonaic sí ach na muca mara ina scuaine
amuigh sa chuan. Do gheit a croí:
is ann a cheap sí gurb iad na beithígh go léir aici féin
a bhí tar éis titim le haill go hobann isteach sa tsruth.
Cheap sí go bhfaigheadh sí leathmharú sa bhaile dá bharr
is do léim suas le teann líonrith agus uamhain
sarar thuig sí cad a bhí suas.
B'shin é an chéad uair a thaibhsigh sé chúichi ar an láthair.

Ina dhiaidh sin
tháinig sé arís is arís chúichi.
Ar dtúis b'ait léi an t-éadach aisteach a bhí air;
an lúireach, na loirgneáin cnámh éisc, is an cafarr,
na lámhainní fada déanta de chraiceann bradán is scadán.
Ní raibh aon oidhre eile air, dar léi, d'fhéadfá a rá,
ach cairictéir neamhdhaonna éigin ó Bh-scannán: –
'An Créatúir ón Lagún Gorm' nó fiú King Kong.
Ach nuair a bhain sé do an clogad a bhí ar a cheann
is chraith a mhoing bhreá ruainní anuas ar a ghualainn,
chonaic sí go soiléir ansin gurbh fhear óg a bhí ann.

Ansan tháinig lá
gur chuir sé a cheann ina hucht.
Bhí na míolta móra ag búirthíl thíos fúthu faoi loch
is na muca mara ina dtáinte gléigeala mórthimpeall.
(Sa tháthnóna thiar
do chonaic daoine a bhí ar an gcnoc le ba iad.)
Is i dteanga éigin iasachta a thuig sí
cé nárbh fhéidir léi na focail a dhéanamh amach i gceart,

d'iarr sé uirthi a cheann a ghlanadh
is na míola a bhí ag crá an chinn air a chnagadh
lena hingne fada.

Do dhein sí amhlaidh.
Bhí sí ag portaireacht go bog faoina hanáil
is í á bhréagadh nuair a baineadh aisti an phreab
is gheit a croí uirthi; bhí dúlamán is duileascar cloch
ag fás i measc rútaí na gruaige aige.
Thuig sí láithreach cad a bhí suas
is nár mhaith an earra é. Ansan
nuair a bhraith sí barraí na gcluas aige thuig sí leis
nach ar Labhraidh Lorc amháin sa scéal
a bhí na cluasa capaill.

Cé gur bhrúcht brat fuarallais trína craiceann amach
do bhain sí míotóg amháin nó dhó nó trí
as a cromán is ní dúirt sí faic.
Lean sí uirthi ar feadh an ama ag cíoradh a chinn,
ag crónán is ag portaireacht,
ag gabháilt de shuantraithe is de ghiotaí beaga amhrán,
á bhréagadh is á mhealladh de shíor chun suain.
Ansan nuair a bhraith sí faid osnaíle
ag teacht ina anáil,
do scaoil sí snaidhmanna a haprúin
go cúramach is go mear

is thug dos na bonnaibh é.
Rith sí ins na tréinte tríd an bhfaill
go tigh a muintire. Ar dtuís
is slaod gibirise amháin i dtaobh rútaí feamnaí
is cluasa capaill a d'eascair as a béal. Ar deireadh
nuair a tuigeadh le deacaireacht agus faoi dheoidh
do lucht an tí cad a bhí á rá aici, d'aithníodar láithreach
is ar an bpointe boise gurb é an t-each uisce é.
D'éiríodar is d'fháisc suas orthu a gcuid balcaisí,
a bhfearas airm is a n-éide catha,
is ritheadar amach ina mbuíon armtha
ar tí a mharaithe.

174

Bhí seans léi, a dúirt na héinne, ina dhiadh san.
Bhí; agus gur dhóbair di: – aon bharrathuisle amháin,
aon ghníomh ar bith ceataí is bhí sí ite aige,
scun scan, beo beathúch, cnámha agus eile.
Trí lá i ndiaidh na tubaiste
seans go mbeadh a hae, an dá scámhóig aici is na duáin
le piocadh suas acu ar bharra taoide.
B'shin an sórt ainmhí é.
B'fhíor dóibh, do thuig sí san.
Mar sin féin do luigh imeachtaí an lae úd
go trom uirthi.
Do shuigh sí síos ar fhaobhar na faille
lá i ndiaidh lae eile

is í ag cuimhneamh ar loinnir uaithne
na súl bhfiarsceabhach aige a d'fhéach uirthi le fonn
a bhí chomh simplí san is chomh glan, folláin,
ina shlí féin le hampla ocrais;
drithle rithimeach na ngéag donn
is conas a chaolaíodar ina riostaí cúnga
ag rí na láimhe aige.
Thar aon ní eile do chuimhnigh sí ar mheatáin
iallaithe a choirp a bhí chomh haiclí
is chomh teann le bogha i bhfearas. An teannas
a bhí ann, mar a bheadh sprionga tochraiste
a bheadh ar tinneall i gcónaí
is réidh faoi bhráid a athscaoilte.

175

The Water-Horse

At first it was only in her dreams
That he came and lay with her.

On the day
She was supposed to be minding the cows
In Sheep Cove (she was reading Dickens,
The Old Curiosity Shop,
And cows were the last thing on her mind)
She saw the porpoises flocking out in the bay
Her heart almost stopped.
She thought they were her cows, all of them
Fallen at once from the cliff to the water.
She thought she'd get a hammering at home
And she had jumped up in her agitation
Before she saw what the bodies were.
That was the first time he appeared to her there.

And after that
He came to her again and again.
At first his clothing seemed so strange to her:
The breastplate, the fishbone greaves and the casque,
The long gloves made from the skin of eels.
His whole style recalling
The subhuman creatures from B movies:
The Creature from Sheep Cove, or an Irish cousin of King Kong.
But when he took the helmet from his head
And his fine horse's mane loosened on his shoulders
She saw clearly that he was a young man.

Then came the day
He laid his head on her breast.
The sea-creatures were hooting below them on the water
And the porpoises in shining troops around them.
(Later in the evening
They were seen by people out after cows on the mountain.)
And in a foreign tongue she understood
Though she could not properly make out the words,

He asked her to comb his hair
And crush with her long nails
The creatures that were pestering his head.

She did what he asked.
She was humming softly under her breath
Soothing him, when she got the fright
That stopped her heart again: seaweed and rook dilisk
Were growing among the roots of his hair.
She guessed at once what was going on
And that it was bad news. Then
When she felt the tips of his ears she knew
That not only Labhraidh Loirc in the old story
Had ears like a horse's ears.

Yet although the cold sweat was running down her skin
She gave herself a pinch in the thigh
Or two or three, and said nothing.
She went on combing his hair the whole time
Humming and murmuring
Lullabies and scraps of songs
To soothe him and beguile him into sleep
And then when she heard his breathing
Changing to the sighs of a sleeper
She undid the strings of her apron
Gently and quickly

And she ran for it.
She made it up the cliffs in a flash
To the house of her people. At first,
All they could get from her was a streel of nonsense
About seaweed roots and horse's ears. At length,
When her people at home had laboured to make out
The meaning of what she was saying, they knew at once
Right on the spot that it was the water-horse.
They rose up and put on their clothes,
Their battle gear and took their weapons,
And out they went as an armed patrol
To find and kill him.

Afterwards they all said she was lucky.
She was, and it was a near thing: one slip,
One step awry and he'd have swallowed her,
Right down, live and kicking, blood and bones.
Three days after the event
They might have found her liver, a couple of lungs and kidneys
Picked up around the high-tide-mark.
That was the sort of beast he was.
It was true for them, she knew it.
And yet she felt the story of that day
Lie heavy on her.
She'd sit there on the cliff edge
Day after day.

And she thought about the green gleam
In the strange eyes that had looked at her with desire,
That was as simple, clean, clear
In its own way as a hearty hunger:
The rhythmic shining of his brown limbs
And how they narrowed to slim wrists
And the shape of the hands.
More than all else she remembered the muscular
Weave of his body that was tense
And light as a tightened bow. The spring
Wound up, alert, constantly
Ready to be released again.

Translated by Eiléan Ní Chuilleanáin

An Mhurúch san Ospidéal

Dhúisigh sí
agus ní raibh a heireaball éisc ann
nios mó
ach istigh sa leaba léi
bhi an dá rud fada fuar seo.
Ba dhóigh leat gur gaid mhara iad
nó slaimicí feola.

"Mar mhagadh atá siad
ní foláir,
Oiche na Coda Móire.
Tá leath an fhoirinn as a meabhar
le deoch
is an leath eile acu
ró-thugtha do jokeanna.
Mar sin féin is leor
an méid so,"
is do chaith sí an dá rud
amach as an seomra.

Ach seo í an chuid
n'a tuigeann sí; –
conas a thit sí féin ina ndiaidh
"cocs-um-bo-head."
Cé'n bhaint a bhí
ag an dá rud leí
nó cé'n bhaint a bhí aici
leosan?

"Cos í seo atá ceangailte díot
agus ceann eile acu anseo thíos fút.
Cos, cos eile,
a haon, a dó.
Caithfidh tú foghlaim
conas síul leo."

Ins na míosa fada
a lean
n'fheadar ar thit a croí
de réir mar a thit
trácht na coise uirthi,
a háirsi?

179

The Mermaid in the Labour Ward

Something stirred in her:
not the swishing meteor of her fin,
but in the pit of the bed,
a body-long split of ice,
languid as dulse tentacles,
flaccid as fishbait.
"Lord Bless Us, isn't this a hoot

some kind of Night of the Long Knives –
half the staff as pissed as a newt
and the rest of them you couldn't trust
as far as you could throw them
I've had it up to here."
And she upped and yanked the sea-legs
out the door.

The crunch came
when she found herself
head over heels in their wake
were these creatures joined
or was she hinged on to them?

It took the nurse
to give her the low-down
and put her in the picture:
"What you have there, dear,
is called a leg,
and another one to boot.
First leg,
second leg,
left, right,
one goes in front of the other."

It's little wonder
in the long months that followed,
as her instep flattened
and her arches dropped,
if her mind went with them.

Translated by Medbh McGuckian

Na Murúcha ag Ní a gCeann

Ó thugadar cúl na láimhe glan don uisce
ní féidir leo iad féin a fholcadh.
Glanann siad na háraistí le meascán fuail is luaithe
is pinch beag gainimhe tríd
is caithfear a admháil tar éis a bhfaigheann siad dá ndua
gur gléineach a bhíonn síad.

Níonn siad a gcoirp le híle is le rósuisce
is a gceann le seampú tirim
(áhbar saorga a ghaibheann siad ón bpoiticéar),
nó le púdar talcaim.

An uair fhada fhánach
a fhliuchann siad a gceann
is le huisce bog é.
Caitheann siad é a dhéanamh
roimh dul sios don ngréin,
rud go bhfuil ábhar maith leis.

Do bhí bean fadó ann a bhí ag tuargaint lín
is bhí beirt chailíní aici.
Dúirt sí leothu go nífidíst a gceann
nuair a bheadh an t-airnéan déanta.

Siar san oíche a bhí sé sin
is nuair nár thug sí aon bhia dóibh
chuir ceann des na cailíní blúire luaithe ina béal
is an cailín eile roinnt cátha.

Do tháinig an cnag sa doras
san oíche siar
is do labhair an guth ann;
"Luathaigh, luaithaigh, bolg luaithe.
Fágaíg', fágaíg', bolg cátha.
Bolg folamh ar an doras seo láithreach."

Ardaíodh chun siúil bean a'tí agus cailín na luaithe
agus fágadh ar an láthair bean na cátha.

Úsáidtear an scéal seo, fiú sa lá atá inniu ann
chun scanradh an diabhail bhuí
a chur ar na maighdeanacha mara óga.

The Marianne Faithful Hairdo

Having washed their hands of water forever,
they can no longer even have a shower.

They scour the household vessels
with a Fairy Liquid purée of ash and urine,
plus a grain of sand thrown in,
and use so much elbow-grease,
you'd have to give it to them,
they finish up like the TV ads.

They exfoliate with oils in attar of rose
and scrub their scalps with a man-made
dry shampoo supplied by Boots,
or ordinary talc.

The few-and-far-between times
that they wet a hair of their heads,
it's with lukewarm tap water.
Which must be applied before sundown
for the following very good reason:

A while back a local woman
was threshing flax with two girl-helpers,
and would only allow them to wash their hair
when the evening shift was over.

The work went on till late in the night,
and since there was no sign of a break,
one of the girls put a flake of ash in her mouth,
the other a pinch of the chaff.

182

Around midnight there came a knock to the door,
and a voice cried: "Away to hell
with the belly of ash! But spare
the belly of chaff – and straight out the door
with the belly that's empty!"

The woman of the house and the ash-girl
turned into thin air,
leaving the girl of chaff
to tell the tale:

which has been handed down from that day
to this, to put the heart across
the breasts of the teenage mermaids.

Translated by Medbh McGuckian

Rita Ann Higgins

Consumptive in the Library

About you:
you carry a kidney donor card,
not yet filled in,
a St Christopher's round your neck
on a brown shoe lace,
(to ward off demons and politicians),
memories of Sweet Afton,
and the racing page from the *Daily Express*
and an unsociable cough.

About me:
I carry illusions
of becoming a famous poet,
guilt about that one time in Baltinglass,
fear that the lift will stop at Limbo,
a slight touch of sciatica
plus an anthology of the Ulster poets.

Unlike your peers
you will not take warmth
from cold churches or soup kitchens,
instead, for long periods, you will
exasperate would-be poets with illusions,
in the reference room of the Galway County Library.

I started with Heaney,
you started to cough.
You coughed all the way to Ormsby,
I was on the verge of Mahon.

Daunted, I left you the Ulster Poets
to consume or cough at.

I moved to the medical section.

Sunny Side Plucked

We met outside
the seconds chicken
van at the market.

He was very American,
I was very married.

We chatted about
the home-made marmalade
I bought two miles
from home.

He said the eggs were big,
I said he'd been eating
his carrots.

'Do you always buy
seconds chickens?'

'Only when I come late.'

The witch in me
wanted to scramble
his eggs.

The devil in him
wanted to pluck
my chicken.

We parted
with an agreement
written by the eyes.

It's All Because We're Working-Class

for Michael I.

Through them
you could see
no rhyme reason
or gable end;
that coal bag washer
and grass eater
from the Shantalla clinic
prescribed them.

Burn your patch
he said
and be a man;
slip these on
and see into
the souls of men;
and our Ambrose
walked into
the gable end
and his life
was in splinters
thereafter.

All he really needed
was to rest his lazy eye
for a few months
and the wrong eye
would right itself.

It's like having your leg
tied behind your back
for six years
then suddenly have it released
and be told,
go now and breakdance
on a tight-rope.

It's all because we're working-class;
if we lived up in Taylor's Hill
with the coal bag washes
and grass eaters,
do you think for one minute
they would put
them big thick spy-glasses on your child?

Not a tall
not a fuckin' tall;
they'd give ya them film star glasses
with the glitter on them,
just as sure
as all their metallic purple wheelbarrows
have matching cocker spaniels
they would;

fuckin' coal bag washers
and grass eaters
the whole fuckin' lot of them;
and it's all because we're working-class.

She Is Not Afraid of Burglars

for Leland B.

Fear of Husband

It's lunchtime
and he's training the dog again.
He says to the dog in a cross voice,
'Stay there.'
The dog obeys him.

When he goes home
he forgets to leave the cross voice
in the green where he trains his dog
and spits out unwoven troubles
that won't fit in his head.

He says to his wife,
'Stay there.'
His wife obeys him.
She sees how good he is with the dog
and how the dog obeys his cross voice.

She boasts to the locals,
'I would never be afraid of burglars
with my husband in the house.'

The locals, busting for news, ask her,
'Why would you never be afraid of burglars
with your husband in the house?'

She calls a meeting at Eyre Square
for half three that Saturday.
Standing on a chair, wiping her hands
on her apron, she explains.

'One day,' she says, in a cross voice,
'The dog disobeyed my husband
and my husband beat him across the head
with a whip made from horse hair.

That is why I am not afraid of burglars
with my husband in the house.'

The Did-You-Come-Yets of the Western World

When he says to you:
You look so beautiful
you smell so nice –
how I've missed you –
and did you come yet?

It means nothing,
and he is smaller
than a mouse's fart.

Don't listen to him . . .
Go to Annaghdown Pier
with your father's rod.
Don't necessarily hold out
for the biggest one;
oftentimes the biggest ones
are the smallest in the end.

Bring them all home,
but not together.
One by one is the trick;
avoid red herrings and scandal.

Maybe you could take two
on the shortest day of the year.
Time is the cheater here
not you, so don't worry.

Many will bite the usual bait;
they will talk their slippery way
through fine clothes and expensive perfume,
fishing up your independence.

These are
the did-you-come-yets of the western world,
the feather and fin rufflers.
Pity for them they have no wisdom.

Others will bite at any bait.
Maggot, suspender, or dead worm.
Throw them to the sharks.

In time one will crawl
out from under thigh-land.
Although drowning he will say,

'Woman I am terrified, why is this house
shaking?'

And you'll know he's the one.

Be Someone
for Carmel

For Christ's sake,
learn to type
and have something
to fall back on.

Be someone,
make something of yourself,
look at Gertrudo Ganley.

Always draw the curtains
when the lights are on.

Have nothing to do
with the Shantalla gang,
get yourself a right man
with a Humber Sceptre.

For Christ's sake
wash your neck
before going into God's house.

Learn to speak properly,
always pronounce your ings.
Never smoke on the street,
don't be caught dead
in them shameful tight slacks,

spare the butter,
economise,

and for Christ's sake
at all times,
watch your language.

Witch in the Bushes

for Padraic Frace

I know a man
who tried
to eat a rock
a big rock
grey and hard,
unfriendly too.

Days later
he is still grinding,
the rock
is not getting
any smaller.

Because of this
rock in the jaw,
this impediment,
the man has become
even more angry.

No one
could look at him,
but a few
hard cases did.
They were mostly dockers;
they reckoned,

'We have seen
the savage seas
rise over our dreams,
we can look
at a bull-head
eating a rock.'

The years passed
slowly and painfully,
until one day

the rock was no more,
neither was much of the man.

He didn't
grind the rock down,
the rock
hammered a job
on him and his ego.

Then, one day
an old woman
came out of the bushes
wearing a black patch
and a questionnaire,
in her wand hand
she held a posh red pencil,
well pared.

She questioned him
between wheezes
(she had emphysema
from smoking damp tobacco
and inhaling fumes
from her open fire
in the woods)
if all that anger
for all those years
was worth it.

Old Rockie Jaw
couldn't answer
he had forgotten
the reason
and the cause.

He concluded
'Anger is OK
if you spill it,
but chewing

is assuredly
murder on the teeth.'

He had learned
his lesson
he would
pull himself together
smarten up like,
turn the other cheek,
he would go easy
on the oils that aged him.

Every now and then
he weakened,
he let the voice
from the rock take over,
an army voice
with a militant tone,

'A man is a man
and a real man
must spit feathers
when the occasion arises.'

Like all good voices
this one
had an uncle,
it was the voice
of the uncle
that bothered him,
it always
had the same warning,

'About
the witch in the bushes,'
it said,
'Watch her,
she never sleeps.'

Anything Is Better than Emptying Bins

for Jessie

I work at the Post Office.
I hate my job,
but my father said
there was no way
I could empty bins
and stay under his roof.

So naturally,
I took a ten week
extra-mural course
on effective stamp-licking;
entitled
'More lip and less tongue.'

I was mostly unpleasant,
but always under forty
for young girls
who bought stamps with hearts
for Valentine's Day.

One day a woman asked me
could she borrow a paper-clip,
she said something about
sending a few poems away
and how a paper-clip
would make everything so much neater.

But I've met the make-my-poems-neater-type before;
give in to her once,
and she'll be back in a week asking,
'Have you got any stamps left over?'

Well I told her where to get off.
'Mrs Neater-poems,' I said,
'this is a Post Office

not a friggin' card shop,
and if you want paper-clips
you'll get a whole box full
across the street for twenty pence.'

Later when I told my father,
he replied,
'Son, it's not how I'd have handled it,
but anything is better than emptying bins.'

Some People
for Eom

Some people know what it's like,

to be called a cunt in front of their children
to be short for the rent
to be short for the light
to be short for school books
to wait in Community Welfare waiting-rooms full of smoke
to wait two years to have a tooth looked at
to wait another two years to have a tooth out (the same tooth)
to be half strangled by your varicose veins, but you're
198th on the list
to talk into a banana on a jobsearch scheme
to talk into a banana in a jobsearch dream
to be out of work
to be out of money
to be out of fashion
to be out of friends
to be in for the Vincent de Paul man
to be in space for the milk man
(sorry, mammy isn't in today she's gone to Mars for the
        weekend)
to be in Puerto Rico this week for the blanket man
to be in Puerto Rico next week for the blanket man
to be dead for the coal man
(sorry, mammy passed away in her sleep, overdose of coal
in the teapot)
to be in hospital unconscious for the rent man
(St Judes ward 4th floor)
to be second-hand
to be second-class
to be no class
to be looked down on
to be walked on
to be pissed on
to be shat on

and other people don't.

200

Philomena's Revenge

As a teenager
she was like any other,
boys, the craic,
smoking down the backs.

Later there was talk
she broke things,
furniture and glass,
her mother's heart.

'Mad at the world,'
the old women nod,
round each other's faces.

But it was more
than that
and for less
she was punished.

That weekend
she didn't leave a cup alone
every chair hit the wall,
Philomena's revenge.

Soon after
she was shifted
and given the shocks.

Round each other's faces
the old women nod
'Treatment, treatment
they've given her the treatment.'

These days
she gets on with the furniture,
wears someone else's walk,
sees visions in glass.

She's good too
for getting the messages;
small things, bread and milk
sometimes the paper,

and closing the gate
after her father drives out,
she waits for his signal
he always shouts twice,

'Get the gate Philo,
get the gate, girl.'

Misogynist

Is the boss in?
Could he give us
a yard of a tow,

the engine's after
collapsin' on me again,
she is, the bitch.

The Deserter

He couldn't wait
just up and died
on me.

Two hours,
two hours
I spent ironing
them shirts
and he didn't even
give me the pleasure
of dirtying them,

that's the type
of person he was,
would rather die
than please you.

But in his favour
I will say this for him,
he made a lovely corpse.
Looked better dead
than he did in our front room
before the telly,

right cock-of-the-walk
in that coffin,
head slightly tilted back
like he was going to say
'My dear people.'

He couldn't wait,
never,
like the time
before the All-Ireland
we were going to Mass,

*Male
abuse /
oppressed*

203

he had to have a pint
or he'd have the gawks, he said.
That's the type he was,
talk dirty in front of any woman.

No stopping him
when he got that ulcer out,
but where did it get him,

wax-faced above
in the morgue
that's where.

He's not giving
out to me now
for using Jeyes Fluid
on the kitchen floor,

or stuffing the cushions
with his jaded socks . . .
and what jaded them?
Pub crawling jaded them,
that's what.

He's tight-lipped now
about my toe separators,
before this
he would threaten them
on the hot ash.

The next time
I spend two hours
ironing shirts for him
he'll wear them.

Old Timers

She loves the clockman;
she leans on his shoulder
from her bicycle,
cycling slowly
through a field.

Slightly out of step,
the botched hip job
leaves him
one foot shorter
than the other.

She adores him;
his slight tick-over
his offbeat with time
but never with her heart.

Children have worn a path
for these older lovers,
harmony not always seen,
the eye is good
but the heart is better.

They're heading for the pub now.
She loves the clockman;
she leans on his shoulder
from her bicycle.

On their return,
his short step less noticeable,
harmony more visible
as the falling together starts.

The treasured bicycle
now takes third place;
it trails like an unwanted relative,
uncle somebody.

When they hit home
he'll make the tea,
he'll rub her old feet,
they'll make yes and no sentences
for ages with love,

and if the voice is good
she'll sing out to her clockman
sweet youthful melodies,

making him forget
years, months, days,
minutes, seconds,
ticks, tocks,

until the only down-to-earth sound
is the click of her new teeth
as she whispers, gently,

'Love, oh love,
there's no time like the present.'

The Flute Girl's Dialogue

Plato, come out now
with your sunburnt legs on ya
don't tell me to play to myself
or to the other women.

'Discourse in Praise of Love' indeed.

Bad mannered lot,
even if I cough when I come into the room
it does not stop your bleating.
That couch over there seats two comfortably
yet every time I enter
there's four of you on it
acting the maggot

then if Socrates walks in,
the way you all suck up to him.

Small wonder Plato
you have a leg to stand on
after all the red herrings
you put in people's mouths.
You hide behind Eryximachus
and suspend me like tired tattle.

'Tell the Flute Girl to go' indeed.

Let me tell you Big Sandals
the Flute Girl's had it.
When I get the sisters in here
we are going to sit on the lot of you,
come out then gushing platonic.

The Flute Girl knows
the fall of toga tune
the flick of tongue
salt-dip hemlock-sip
eye to the sky tune
hand on the thigh tune
moan and whimper talk
dual distemper talk.

When you played I listened,
when I play, prick up your ears.

Remapping the Borders

In Texas
after the conference
they put on a céilí,
nearly everyone danced,
a few of us Margarita'd.

In jig time
everyone knew everyone.
After the Siege of Ennis
a woman asked me,
'Could you see my stocking belt
as I did the swing?'

I was taken aback.

Me, thigh, knee, no,
I saw nothing.
I saw no knee
no luscious thigh
no slither belt,
with lace embroidered border
that was hardly a border at all.

I was looking for the worm in my glass.

I thought about her after,
when I was high above St Louis.
I'm glad I didn't see
her silk white thighs
her red satin suspender belt
with black embroidered border
that was hardly a border at all.

I swear to you
I saw nothing,
not even the worm
lying on his back
waiting to penetrate my tongue.

Night Noon and Nora

He was dead
no two ways about it
only his bones
never hit the clay
they were home
hitting the roof
when visitors came
he didn't want company
he only wanted her
not to leave him
to his thoughts
and his tea-stained eyes.

Master of mime,
he put on fantasy stockings
he sat on fantasy chairs
he called her
night noon and Nora,
the woman he nearly married
forty years ago
the woman whose husband Pious
got back cancer
from carrying her troubles.

He went for a spoon
and he brought back a fish.
Once at Eyre Square, he cried,
'I don't know who I am
promise you'll never leave me Nora
even when I'm asleep.'

Her word was gospel,
she got tired nodding
but she never slept,
except for the forty winks last September.
She remembered every wink
like thick soup, she said.

She went to grief councillors,
she told them
bones in the house
spirit in the sky
stockings that aren't there
chairs that are no chairs
fish that are spoons
he's calling me Nora
I'm Bridget on the brink of a breakdown
help me.

They told her to let go
and let ever loving God
do night watchman.

The last straw was when
he turned up at second Mass
wearing only a lost look,
his clothes were at home
on the back of a chair,
a real chair.

She screamed out
to her ever loving God,
'I'm Bridget on the brink of a breakdown,
deliver me.'

God wasn't in at the time
he was down in Middle Street
making mince meat out of Pious's cancer,
everyone knew that.

Paula Meehan

The Leaving

He had fallen so far down into himself
I couldn't reach him.
Though I had arranged our escape
he wouldn't budge. He sat
days in his room checking manuscripts

or fixing photos of his family
strictly in the order they were taken.
I begged him hurry for
the moonless nights were due;
it was two nights' walk through the forest.

The soldiers had recently entered our quarter.
I dreaded each knock on the door,
their heavy boots on the stairs.
Our friends advised haste;
many neighbours were already in prison.

His eyes were twin suns burning.
Silence was his answer to my pleas.
I packed a change of clothes, half
the remaining rations,
my mother's gold ring for barter.

The documents at a glance would pass.
It wasn't for myself I went but
for the new life I carried.
At the frontier I recalled him – that last morning
by the window watching the sun

strut the length of the street, mirroring
the clouds' parade. He wore
the black shirt I'd embroidered with stars
and said nothing. Nothing.
Then the guide pushed me forward.

Between one sweep of the searchlight
and the next, I slipped into another state
gratefully, under the cover of darkness.

Zugzwang

She fills jugs of water at the sink
for flowers: mignonette, cotton lavender,
for their scent and fretty form,
sweet pea and love-lies-bleeding,
a token of domestic tragedy, a wound.

He looks up from the chessboard where
he's replaying a famous game of Capablanca's.
He catches her off guard, murmuring
to herself, framed by the door, the blooms.
She wears a dress for a change,
of a sea blue that ebbs to green
when sun floods the kitchen.
Beyond is the window. The sky is an ocean
where clouds like spacecraft or cuban cigars
float towards the mountain.
He imagines Dutch paintings, bourgeois
interiors, *Woman Washing*, *Woman Setting
a Table*, *Woman Bending over a Child*
and conjures a painting half made –
Woman Surrounded by Flowers at a Sink,
himself at an easel mixing pigment and oil,
a north facing studio above a canal
where barges are waiting their turn at the lock
and on the Zuyder Zee scuppy waves rock sailboats.
The landscape surrenders to a polar light.

She arranges the flowers in two jugs.
Lately she has heard her dead mother's voice
tumbling in the drier with the wash:
I told you so, I told you so, I told you so.
The women on the TV in their business suits
and white teeth transmit coded messages,
escape maps buried in their speeches,
though they appear to be reading the news
lest others are watching. Soldiers
have set up a barricade down the road;

they are part of a nationwide search
for a desperate man and his hostage.

A jug in each hand, she moves to the table
and he fancies she has stepped straight into
a Cretan mosaic, a priestess in a Minoan rite,
devotee of the bull, and himself a mosaic worker
fingering a thousand fragments until he finds
the exact shade of blue with that green undertow
to fit his pattern. For her face
and breasts he would use tiles of pure gold;
the alchemists hold it has the exact
calibration of human skin. He will not dwell

on last week's events when he woke
in the night and she was gone. He found her
digging in the garden, her nightgown
drenched through, muck smeared on her arms,
on her legs, the rain lashing down.
She explained that she wanted to be close
to her loved ones, her lost ones, that
they are so cold and lonely in the earth
and they long for the warmth of the living.

She places the flowers on the table.
Any day now she will let go her grip,
surrender herself to the ecstatic freefall.
We are all aware that when she hits bottom
she will shatter into smithereens.
Each shard will reflect the room, the flowers,
the chessboard, and her beloved sky beyond
like a calm ocean lapping at the mountain.

Buying Winkles

My mother would spare me sixpence and say,
'Hurry up now and don't be talking to strange
men on the way.' I'd dash from the ghosts
on the stairs where the bulb had blown
out into Gardiner Street, all relief.
A bonus if the moon was in the strip of sky
between the tall houses, or stars out,
but even in rain I was happy – the winkles
would be wet and glisten blue like little
night skies themselves. I'd hold the tanner tight
and jump every crack in the pavement,
I'd wave up to women at sills or those
lingering in doorways and weave a glad path through
men heading out for the night.

She'd be sitting outside the Rosebowl Bar
on an orange-crate, a pram loaded
with pails of winkles before her.
When the bar doors swung open they'd leak
the smell of men together with drink
and I'd see light in golden mirrors.
I envied each soul in the hot interior.

I'd ask her again to show me the right way
to do it. She'd take a pin from her shawl –
'Open the eyelid. So. Stick it in
till you feel a grip, then slither him out.
Gently, mind.' The sweetest extra winkle
that brought the sea to me.
'Tell yer Ma I picked them fresh this morning.'

I'd bear the newspaper twists
bulging fat with winkles
proudly home, like torches.

The Pattern

Little has come down to me of hers,
a sewing machine, a wedding band,
a clutch of photos, the sting of her hand
across my face in one of our wars

when we had grown bitter and apart.
Some say that's the fate of the eldest daughter.
I wish now she'd lasted till after
I'd grown up. We might have made a new start

as women without tags like *mother, wife*
sister, daughter, taken our chances from there.
At forty-two she headed for god knows where.
I've never gone back to visit her grave.

      *

First she'd scrub the floor with Sunlight soap,
an armreach at a time. When her knees grew sore
she'd break for a cup of tea, then start again
at the door with lavender polish. The smell
would percolate back through the flat to us,
her brood banished to the bedroom.

And as she buffed the wax to a high shine
did she catch her own face coming clear?
Did she net a glimmer of her true self?
Did her mirror tell what mine tells me?
I have her shrug and go on
knowing history has brought her to her knees.

She'd call us in and let us skate around
in our socks. We'd grow solemn as planets
in an intricate orbit about her.

      *

She's bending over crimson cloth,
the younger kids are long in bed.
Late summer, cold enough for a fire,
she works by fading light
to remake an old dress for me.
It's first day back at school tomorrow.

                    *

'Pure lambswool. Plenty of wear in it yet.
You know I wore this when I went out with your Da.
I was supposed to be down in a friend's house,
your Granda caught us at the corner.
He dragged me in by the hair – it was long as yours then –
in front of the whole street.
He called your Da every name under the sun,
cornerboy, lout; I needn't tell you
what he called me. He shoved my whole head
under the kitchen tap, took a scrubbing brush
and carbolic soap and in ice-cold water he scrubbed
every spick of lipstick and mascara off my face.
Christ but he was a right tyrant, your Granda.
It'll be over my dead body anyone harms a hair of your head.'

                    *

She must have stayed up half the night
to finish the dress. I found it airing at the fire,
three new copybooks on the table and a bright
bronze nib, St Christopher strung on a silver wire,

as if I were embarking on a perilous journey
to uncharted realms. I wore that dress
with little grace. To me it spelt poverty,
the stigma of the second hand. I grew enough to pass

it on by Christmas to the next in line. I was sizing
up the world beyond our flat patch by patch
daily after school, and fitting each surprising
city street to city square to diamond. I'd watch

the Liffey for hours pulsing to the sea
and the coming and going of ships,
certain that one day it would carry me
to Zanzibar, Bombay, the Land of the Ethiops.

    *

There's a photo of her taken in the Phoenix Park
alone on a bench surrounded by roses
as if she had been born to formal gardens.
She stares out as if unaware
that any human hand held the camera, wrapped
entirely in her own shadow, the world beyond her
already a dream, already lost. She's
eight months pregnant. Her last child.

    *

Her steel needles sparked and clacked,
the only other sound a settling coal
or her sporadic mutter
at a hard part in the pattern.
She favoured sensible shades:
Moss Green, Mustard, Beige.

I dreamt a robe of a colour
so pure it became a word.

Sometimes I'd have to kneel
an hour before her by the fire,
a skein around my outstretched hands,
while she rolled wool into balls.
If I swam like a kite too high
amongst the shadows on the ceiling
or flew like a fish in the pools
of pulsing light, she'd reel me firmly
home, she'd land me at her knees.

Tongues of flame in her dark eyes,
she'd say, 'One of these days I must
teach you to follow a pattern.'

219

Child Burial

Your coffin looked unreal,
fancy as a wedding cake.

I chose your grave clothes with care,
your favourite stripey shirt,

your blue cotton trousers.
They smelt of woodsmoke, of October,

your own smell there too.
I chose a gansy of handspun wool,

warm and fleecy for you. It is
so cold down in the dark.

No light can reach you and teach you
the paths of wild birds,

the names of the flowers,
the fishes, the creatures.

Ignorant you must remain
of the sun and its work,

my lamb, my calf, my eaglet,
my cub, my kid, my nestling,

my sucking, my colt. I would spin
time back, take you again

within my womb, your amniotic lair,
and further spin you back

through nine waxing months
to the split seeding moment

you chose to be made flesh,
word within me.

I'd cancel the love feast
the hot night of your making.

I would travel alone
to a quiet mossy place,

you would spill from me into the earth
drop by bright red drop

Return and No Blame

Father of mine,
your sunny smile
is a dandelion
as I come once again through the door.

Our fumbled embrace
drives the wind off my shoulder
and your eyes hold a question
you will not put
as I break bread at your table
after the long seasons away from it.

Father, my head is bursting
with the things I've seen
in this strange, big world

but I don't have the words to tell you
nor the boldness to disrupt your gentle daily ways,
so I am quiet while the rashers cook,
nod and grin at any old thing.

'Oh, the boat was grand,
they took me in at Larne.'
'And a pity they didn't keep you.
Must have been a gypsy slipped you in
and I in a dead sleep one night.'

Didn't I rob you of your eyes, father,
and her of her smile? No dark blood
but the simple need to lose an uneasy love
drove me down unknown roads
where they spoke in different tongues,
drove me about the planet
till I had of it
and it of me
what we needed of each other.

Yes, father, I will have more tea
and sit here quiet in this room of my childhood
and watch while the flames flicker
the story of our distance on the wall.

Her Heroin Dream

She dreamt the moon a gaudy egg,
a Chinese gimcrack. When it hatched,
a young dragon would spiral to earth
trailing garnet and emerald sparks,
shrieking through the ozone layer,
the citizens blinded by dragon-glory.

In the heart of night would blaze a light
greater than the sun, supernova fierce.

The Liffey and the two canals would vanish
and Dublin bay evaporate, leaving beached
spiny prawns and crabs, coiled sea snails,
a dead sailor's shoe, shipping wrecks,
radioactive waste in Saharas of sand.
The buildings would scorch to black stumps,
windows melt, railroads buckle,
bricks fallen to dust would sift
in dervish swirls along the thoroughfares.

Each tree in the town would turn torch
to celebrate his passing.

She would wait in her cell.
He'd enter softly in the guise of a youth:
his eyes the blue of hyacinth,
his skin like valerian,
his lips Parthian red.
He'd take her from behind.

The kundalini energy would shoot straight up her spine,
blow her head open like a flower.
Dragon seed would root deep in her womb.
Dragon nature course through her veins.

They'd slip from the cell hands twined,
glide over the prison wall into a new morning
to sport among the ruins.

Fruit

Alone in the room
with the statue of Venus
I couldn't resist
Cupping her breast.

It was cool
and heavy in my hand
like an apple.

The Man Who Was Marked by Winter

He was heading for Bridal Veil Falls,
an upward slog on a dusty path.
Mid May and hot as a mill-

stone grinding his shoulders, his back.
Each breath was a drowning.
And who's to say if it was a mirage

the other side of the creek's brown
water. He saw it, that's enough,
in the deep shade of a rocky overhang –

the spoor of winter, a tracery of ice. If
we'd reached him, we'd have warned him of the depth,
the secret current underneath.

He must have been half crazy with the heat.
He stripped off. Waded in.
His feet were cut from under him. He was swept

downriver in melt water from the mountain.
She clutched him to her breast, that beast of winter.
One look from her agate eyes and he abandoned

hope. He was pliant. She pulled him under.
If she had him once, she had him thrice.
She shook his heart and mind asunder.

And he would willingly have gone back to her palace
or her lair, whichever; whatever she was,
he would have lived forever in her realms of ice.

She must have grown tired of his human ways.
We found him tossed like a scrap on the bank,
hours or years or seconds later. His eyes

stared straight at the sun. His past is a blank
snowfield where no one will step. She made her mark
below his heart, a five-fingered gash – *Bondsman*.

My Love about His Business in the Barn

You're fiddling with something in the barn,
a makeshift yoke for beans to climb,
held together like much in our lives
with blue baling twine, scraps of chicken wire.

Such a useless handyman: our world could collapse,
frequently *has* with a huff and a puff.
You'd hoke a length of string from your back pocket,
humming a Woody Guthrie song, you'd bind

the lintel to stone, the slate to rafter,
'It'll do for the minute if the wind stays down.'
And so I've learned to live with dodgy matter:
shelves that tumble to the floor if you glance

at them sideways; walls that were not built
for leaning against; a great chasm in the kitchen
crossable only by a rope bridge; a blow hole
by our bed where the Atlantic spouts.

On stormy nights it drenches the walls, the ceiling.
Days you come home reeking of *Brut* and brimstone
I suspect you've been philandering underground
and not breaking your back beyond on the bog.

So is it any wonder when I see you
mooching in the barn this fine May morning,
a charm of finches lending local colour,
that I rush for my holy water, my rabbit's foot?

That I shut my eyes tight and wait
for the explosion, then the silence,
then the sweet aftershock when the earth skids
under me, when stars and deep space usurp my day?

Laburnum

You walk into an ordinary room
on an ordinary evening, say
mid May, when the laburnum

hangs over the railings of the Square
and the city is lulled by eight o'clock,
the traffic sparse, the air fresher.

You expect to find someone
waiting, though now you live
alone. You've answered none

of your calls. The letters pile
up in the corner. The idea
persists that someone waits while

you turn the brass handle and knock
on the light. Gradually
the dark seeps into the room, you lock

out the night, scan a few books.
It's days since you ate.
The plants are dying – even the cactus,

shrivelled like an old scrotum,
has given up the ghost. There's
a heel of wine in a magnum

you bought, when? The day
before? The day before that?
It's the only way

out. The cold sweats
begin. You knock back a few.
You've no clean clothes left.

He is gone. Say it.
Say it to yourself, to the room.
Say it loud enough to believe it.

You will live breath
by breath. The beat of your own heart
will scourge you. You'll wait

in vain, for he's gone from you.
And every night is a long
slide to the dawn you

wake to, terrified in your ordinary room
on an ordinary morning, say
mid May, say the time of laburnum.

'Would you jump into my grave as quick?'

Would you jump into my grave as quick?
my granny would ask when one of us took
her chair by the fire. You, woman,
done up to the nines, red lips a come on,
your breath reeking of drink
and your black eye on my man tonight
in a Dublin bar, think
first of the steep drop, the six dark feet.

Dream Filter

Before you were born,
I made a dream filter
to ensure you clear dreamings

for the whole of your childhood,
to the exact specifications
of a tribe I read about

in *National Geographic*. First
I'd to clear my own dreams
and pass all my bad visions

into stones; then go on foot
to pure swift running water
near where it entered the sea

and cast each weighted stone
to the pebbly bed
where they could be washed to a calm

stonedness again. Only
then was I fit to begin.

     *

The finding of coppiced hazel,
the twisting of hempen twine,
the building of the dream filter

itself, took a full seven months.
Wait for a bird
to gift you some feathers.

On the walk to the hospital
down by the South Docks,
after a night spent in labour,

three slate-grey feathers there in my path.
I looked up and saw
a peregrine falcon hung in the air –

one of a pair that were nesting
on top of the gasometer.

     *

This contraption
made of hazel and hemp
and a few tail feathers

is fixed tonight above your cradle.
One day you'll ask
what it's all about.

And what can I tell you?
What can I possibly say?

Moya Cannon

Thirst in the Burren

No ground or floor
is as kind to the human step
as the rain-cut flags
of these white hills.

Porous as skin,
limestone resounds sea-deep, time-deep
yet, in places, rainwater has worn it thin
as a fish's fin.

From funnels and clefts
ferns arch their soft heads.

A headland full of water, dry as bone,
with only thirst as a diviner,
thirst of the inscrutable fern
and the human thirst
that beats upon a stone.

Oar

Walk inland and inland
with your oar,
until someone asks you
what it is.

Then build your house.

For only then will you need to tell and know
that the sea is immense and unfathomable,
that the oar that pulls
against the wave
and with the wave
is everything.

Scar

Why does it affect
and comfort me
the little scar
where, years ago, you cut your lip
shaving when half drunk
and in a hurry
to play drums in public.

We step now
to rhythms we don't own or understand,
and, with blind, dog-like diligence,
we hunt for scars
in tender places.

Crannóg

Where an ash bush grows in the lake
a ring of stones has broken cover
in this summer's drought.
Not high enough to be an island,
it holds a disc of stiller water
in the riffled lake.

Trees have reclaimed the railway line behind us;
behind that, the road goes east –
as two lines parallel in space and time run away from us
this discovered circle draws us in.
In drowned towns
bells toll only for sailors and for the credulous
but this necklace of wet stones,
remnant of a wattle Atlantis,
catches us all by the throat.

We don't know what beads or blades
are held in the bog lake's wet amber
but much of us longs to live in water
and we recognise this surfacing
of old homes of love and hurt.

A troubled bit of us is kin
to people who drew a circle in water,
loaded boats with stone,
and raised a dry island and a fort
with a whole lake for a moat.

Oysters

There is no knowing,
or hardly any,
more wondering –
for no one knows what joy the stone holds
in its stone heart,
or whether the lark is full of sorrow
as it springs against the sky.
What do we know, for instance,
of the ruminations of the oyster
which lies on the estuary bed –
not the rare, tormented pearl-maker,
just the ordinary oyster?
Does it dream away its years?

Or is it hard,
this existence where salt and river water mix?
The endless filtering
to sustain a pale silky life,
the labouring to build a grey shell,
incorporating all that floods and tides push in its way,
stones, mud, the broken shells of other fish.

Perhaps the oyster does not dream or think or feel at all
but then how can we understand
the pull of that huge muscle beside the heart
which clamps the rough shell shut
before a hunting starfish or a blade
but which opens it
to let in the tide?

Tending

When a wood fire burns down and falls apart
the fire in each log dies quickly
unless burnt ends are tilted together –
a moment's touch, recognition;
gold and blue flame
wraps the singing wood.

Arctic Tern

Love has to take us unawares
for none of us would pay love's price if we knew it.
For who will pay to be destroyed?
The destruction is so certain,
so evident.

Much harder to chart,
less evident,
is love's second life,
a tern's egg,
revealed and hidden
in a nest of stones
on a stony shore.

What seems a stone
is no stone.
This vulnerable pulse
which could be held in the palm of a hand
may survive
to voyage the world's warm and frozen oceans,
its tapered wings,
the beat of its small heart,
a span between arctic poles.

Milk

Could he have known
that any stranger's baby
crying out loud in a street
can start the flow?
A stain that spreads
on fustian
or denim.

This is kindness
which in all our human time
has refused to learn propriety,
which still knows nothing
but the depth of kinship,
the depth of thirst.

Scríob

Start again from nothing and scrape
since scraping is now part of us;
the sheep's track, the plough's track
are marked into the page,
the pen's scrape cuts a path on the hill.

But today I brought back
three bones of a bird,
eaten before it was hatched
and spat or shat out with its own broken shell
to weather on the north cliffs of Hoy.

This is an edge
where the pen runs dumb.
The small bleached bones of a fulmar or gannet
have nothing to tell.
They have known neither hunger nor flight
and have no understanding of the darkness
which came down and killed.

Tracks run to an end,
sheep get lost in the wet heather.
There are things which can neither be written, nor spoken,
    nor read;
thin wing bones which cannot be mended.

Too fragile for scraping,
the bones hold in their emptiness
the genesis of the first blown note.

Thole-Pin

Who speaks of victory? Endurance is all.
    – Rainer Maria Rilke

Words, old tackle

obsolete tools
moulder in outhouses, sheds of the mind –
the horse-collar rots on a high hook;
a flat-iron and an open razor rust together.

Sometimes a word is kept on
at just one task, its hardest,
in the corner of some trade or skill.
Thole survives,
a rough dowel
hammered into a boat's gunnel
to endure –
a pivot
seared between elements.

Introductions

Some of what we love
we stumble upon –
a purse of gold thrown on the road,
a poem, a friend, a great song.

And more
discloses itself to us –
a well among green hazels,
a nut thicket –
when we are worn out searching
for something quite different.

And more
comes to us, carried
as carefully
as a bright cup of water,
as new bread.

239

Driving Through Light in West Limerick

Poetry,
surpassing music, must take the place
of empty heaven and its hymns.
        – Wallace Stevens

What's light that falls on nothing?
Nothing.
But this light turns wet trees into green lamps
and roadside grass into a green blaze
and lets the saffron hills run through our hearts
as though the world had no borders
and wet whin bushes were deeper than the sun.

What's light,
and who can hold it?
This morning, across the sea, in a gallery
I saw light held for five hundred years
on an angel's face –
a moment's surprise,
and centuries fell away
quiet as leaves.

But the angel's features
had been no more than any perfect features
until they'd caught the light
or else the light had fallen on them.

And trying to figure out
which had happened
I got off the Underground at King's Cross
and an accordion tune filled
the deep steel stairwell.

This was some descent of the strong sun,
good music
brought down to where it was needed,
music surpassing poetry
gone down again,

the busker with a red *Paolo Soprani*
telling again
of Orpheus in Connacht.

The escalators ground up and down
carrying all the people
up and down a hill
of saffron light.

Hunter's Moon

There are perhaps no accidents,
no coincidences.
When we stumble against people, books, rare moments out
    of time,
these are illuminations –
like the hunter's moon that sails tonight in its high clouds,
casting light into our black harbour,
where four black turf boats
tug at their ropes,
hunger for the islands.

Night

Coming back from Cloghane
in the sudden frost
of a November night,
I was ambushed
by the river of stars.

Disarmed by lit skies
I had utterly forgotten
this arc of darkness,
this black night
where the frost-hammered stars
were notes thrown from a chanter,
crans of light.

So I wasn't ready
for the dreadful glamour of Orion
as he struck out over Barr dTrí gCom
in his belt of stars.

At Gleann na nGealt
his bow of stars
was drawn against my heart.

What could I do?

Rather than drive into a pitch-black ditch
I got out twice,
leaned back against the car
and stared up at our windy, untidy loft
where old people had flung up old junk
they'd thought might come in handy,
ploughs, ladles, bears, lions, a clatter of heroes,
a few heroines, a path for the white cow, a swan
and, low down, almost within reach,
Venus, completely unfazed by the frost.

Mary O'Malley

The Visit

The little girl tightened
the belt on her skimpy
homemade cotton dress,
knowing her clothes marked her,
that even her polished shoes were wrong.
But she smiled as she burned,
shame corseted her frame,
buckled the words
coming out of her mouth,
making even her accent a misshapen thing.

She longed and she hated
but she spoke
every time one of them came
graciously, to visit her mother.

Cornered

As a child, were you dark or fair?
The innocent question gaffed her.

I was a dark child, and frail.
I never warmed to land

but if anyone menaced my shore
I would tooth and claw and nail

for the only thing I had,
an undiscovered continent

of swirly forests and scant
unwinding sheets of sand.

The Price of Silk is Paid in Stone

O sweet romance in Connemara!
A soft day, a speckled hill,
a mirror bay, all certain
as the mountains swollen with heather.
All transient as thrushes' eggs,
the wild water
and a streaked chameleon sky.

O no romance in Connemara.
A speckled hen
fasting under a basket,
a whetted knife and the danse macabre,
the musk of feathers in the Sunday stew.

Yes, and when you lack the guts
to wield the knife
what use is it to the hungry child
that you dwell in gossamer and dusk?
Let them find out early
that love has a bitter edge
when life is lived among the rocks.

Yet I have seen the sedge
burn with slow fire.
I have seen the lakes rise
and make swirls of silk
in the October sky.

O the price of leaving,
the cost of coming home.

The Cave

What shades will enter my dark cave tonight?
Who will the moon render powerless or strong?
What shapes? The fuss and tumble
of a Hollywood battle scene?
An unshriven soul, thin and white?
Sea virgins might even now be swimming in
with those grey ancestors of the Mac Conghaile,
the seals. The toss and tangle of shawled women
settling in for the long haul is certain.

Certain the dark hours falling silently
off all the precarious roofs of dreams,
frantic in the web of dream's unquiet authority.
Those shrill or whispering ghosts
the ancestral dead, enter nightly
claiming to be heard. They thresh the straits
of broad and slender vowels, choking on words.
My mouth is wracked like a poem
stretched between spark and shape.

'Caol le caol agus leathan le leathan'[1] mocks me.
I listen to the seals' sweet haunt
and trace its provenance. It shocks the ear.
Are these the trapped voices of the drowned
or is it the strange cry of dumb creatures
longing for something more, to be human?
Like ourselves. Always we are doomed.
I cannot put English on this,
the song of unattainable things, so I hum.

I have always lived by a sea cave
where a dark man waits, incurious.
His face, half-hidden, half-seen
is like the incipient moon, unmoved

1. A spelling rule in Irish

and like the moon he watches the night unfold.
Useless to expect rescue but nonetheless
we expect it. Light. A flame
slowly turned up like an oil lamp,
eyes kindled by a swell of lost radiance.

In light the shawled women shrivel,
their incessant watching requires a veil.
The dark man, illumined is unmasked.
Once would be enough. One deep kiss
of light to eclipse the last pool of darkness
in Europe[2] and all sink back into shadow
rested, confirmed that tomorrow
will be glorious. The wait is ancient;
no God has risen from this cold sea yet.

Yet, on nights when the sky plunders
the last drops of light from the water
and waves, innocent with tangled seaweed
suck and mutter in the cave, remember
that not far from here a man broke faith;
in need of ballast for his boat
he took the chapel stones from a sacred island.
Later, heaving them overboard uneasily
he looked back and saw the stolen rocks float.

2. The philosopher Wittgenstein referred to
Connemara as "the last pool of darkness in Europe."

Cealtrach

The children were never told
about those places. The unbreachable
silence of women protected us
from terrible things.
We heard the dread whisperings
and peopled the swarming spaces with ghosts.

Yet we never knew. They buried
unnamed innocents by the sea's edge
and in the unchurched graveyards
that straddled boundary walls. Those infants
half-human, half-soul were left
to make their own way on the night shore.

Forbidden funerals, where did mothers
do their crying in the two-roomed cottages
so beloved of those Irish times?
Never in front of the living children.
Where then? In the haggard, the cowshed,
the shadowed alcoves of their church?

That Christian religion was hard.
It mortified the flesh
and left mothers lying empty,
their full breasts aching, forever afraid
of what the winter storms might yield,
their own dreams turning on them like dogs.

The Fiddle Player

He cradles the fiddle to his chin
tucking it in like a child
and a hawthorn bends with blackbirds.

As he hefts the bow, tests the air
for sweetness or unremembered ghosts
silver flashes in a clean river.

The bow quivers for an instant,
light as the last sliver of day
over the Corrib; will he make us dance

or draw all our unsaid sorrows
into one lamenting call
to ebb and flow and soothe us?

He strikes the first note;
birds fly, feet tap and three trout
clear the furious waterfall.

Liadan with a Mortgage Briefly Tastes the Stars

Breasting the hill, she pauses and looks down.
In the stillness, her children sleep. She sees lights
winking in Mayo, Croagh Patrick
invisible to the right, her husband inside reading.

The house, anchored at the edge of the world
is solid, comforting. Oh, she thinks,
have we really been our own architects?

The earth gurgles as last night's rain seeps
to its subterranean level.
She would hate to live on dry land.
The house pulses like amber. It is warm
and the weather, settling at last
unsettles her. Those treacherous Septembers!

There are mounds of soft fruit ripening,
waiting to be preserved. She sees
plum and damson staining the clouds. This year
there will be no harvesting. Let those colours
ache and deepen into havoc –
she is not responsible.

A cat whispers past her feet, nightstalking.
She smiles
and sheds her garments, a light blouse and skirt
then slips into the watered sky
and holds it for a moment to her skin,
all moisture
a dress to go wandering out beyond the stars in,
stravaiging among the planets
like Zeus's daughter.
She could take in the whole universe tonight.

The house is oblivious, its roots
pierce the bedrock. Although she is glad
some god made a woman of her
she will acquiesce and go in. She dresses
and walks to her back door, quieted for now.
To the east a garnet moon rises.

The Maighdean Mhara

It is always the same,
the men say little and the women talk,
guessing what the men are saying
in the long gaps between words.
Always fishing for clues
they drop barbs, make humorous casts
in an endless monologue of lures.
They'll say anything for a bite.
The men look hunted and stay silent.

But I can make them sing out
a shower of curses and commands.
I challenge them to win
against the sea and other men.
They listen for the slightest whisper
between me and the wind. They understand
my lightest sigh, and respond.

Here in my belly where men feel safe
I draw out their soft talk,
rising, falling, low as breath.
At ease and sure of their control
they are, in Irish, eloquent.
I never let on anything
but fall and rise and humour them.

Grainne's Answer to Burke's Proposal

Take me for one year certain
hot and cold and strong.
What woman will give you
as much for that long?
A year in a wild place.
Take me or leave me as I am.

The Wound

Nothing changes. The legend tells of three men
In a currach, fishing.
A big sea rose up and threatened to engulf them.

They cast lots to see who was wanted – a young man.
As the swell hung over him
He grabbed a knife and pitched in desperation,

Cold steel against the wave.
The sea withdrew and all were saved.
One man heard a cry of pain and prayed.

At nightfall a woman on a white horse
Enquired and found the house.
'My mistress is sick and only you can save her,'

She said and gave him guarantees.
They took the road under the sea
To a palace where a beautiful woman lay.

His knife was buried in her right breast.
'This is the knife you cast into my flesh.
You must pull it out with a single stroke

Or I will die by midnight.' He did
And the wound became a rose. She offered
The treasures of her green underworld,

A pagan kiss. The same old story. She begged:
'This scar will ache forever if you go.'
Then a choir of lost men whispered

'Stay here and she will have your soul.'
So he blessed himself, refused and went above
To the simple solid world he understood.

Lullaby

Golden nets and silver fish
Floating in the sky,
Lift me on your shoulders Daddy,
Daddy swing me high.

And if the fishes are all tears
And if the nets are dry,
We'll chase the moon with blazing spears
Across the ice-cold sky.
Carry me on your shoulders Daddy,
Daddy swing me high.

Shoeing the Currach

Seventeen feet of canvas
Stretched across the supple hoops of her
And with one deft push of a shoe
She'd spin into his hands
And lightly he'd lift and turn her.

That's how it was with them
Until the balance shifted.
The foot smashed down,
An awkward turn, he can't hold her,
Now she's torn and useless on the sand.

Disgusted, he walks away,
His big hands useless
And no words for what is done.

A Young Matron Dances Free of the Island

One Tuesday in November she finished the wash-up,
Mounted a white horse
And rode into the force nine waves
Out beyond the lighthouse.
Feck it, she said, startling the neighbours,
It's go now or be stuck here forever
Chained to this rock like that Greek,
With the gannets tearing at my liver.

She rode bareback out the roads. The horse reared
But climbed the foothills of the breakers.
When she heard her children calling
Mama, mama, she turned, praying
Jesus, let me make shore
And I will never desert them again,
Nor be ungrateful. When she got in
Half drowned, there was no-one there.

For weeks in the psychiatric all she could see
Were graveyards, men laid out in coffins,
The little satin curtains
They would have shunned in life, of palest ivory
About to be drawn. It was the long winters
They say, drove her out again
To where there was no going back.
She loved parties, was a beautiful dancer –

There is no other explanation.
The husband was good to her, by all accounts.
Does it matter? There should be a moment,
A shard of glass to hold against the light,
A checkpoint to pass before the end.
He has nothing, though people are kind.
They say her hair caught the sun
As she waltzed over the cliff, haloing beautifully down.

The Sea Urchin

She needs the spines
For dignity, her natural resistance
Along faintly bruised lines.
Deep inside the shell she is exposed
And glows or shivers
In her soft pink flesh.
This is also where she cries
With her hundred crescent eyes.

The Seal Woman, v

You can enter the legend anywhere.
On High Street a man is being measured up
For a bainin jacket in Molloy's shop.
There are bolts of swansdown and muslin.
Outside the streets are emptying.

All evening she wanders the estates
Waiting for the moon to rise.
She looks in on an old school friend
Presses her face against the windowpane
And sees her reading to her children.

She looks with envy at the settled women.
Gossiping by the fire.
They make lovely pictures
With husbands and garnet wine,
Candles shattering the crystal.
She would like to join them
But what would she have to talk about?

She knows ordinary women
Half love normal men.
They learn survival, a lukewarm thing,
But this revenge is cold.
For years she scarcely thought of them.
Now it is far too late.

She cups the young moon between her palms
And makes to draw it down. One by one
Hard diamonds glitter in the sky,
Incalculably cold. Look, he once said annoyed,
What the fuck are the stars for anyway?

To be saved there is a task she must perform.
The knives are sharpening in her eyes.
She must shine one more time for him,
Outdo herself this once,
Release the last drops of light
Stored in the amber at her throat.
Then she would bring him down and quench.

Kerry Hardie

We Change the Map

This new map, unrolled, smoothed,
seems innocent as the one we have discarded,
impersonal as the clocks in rows
along the upper border, showing time-zones.

The colours are pale and clear, the contours
crisp, decisive, keeping order.
The new names, lettered firmly, lie quite still
within the boundaries that the wars spill over.

It is the times.

I have always been one for paths myself.
The mole's view. Paths and small roads and the next bend.
Arched trees tunnelling to a coin of light.
No overview, no sense of what lies where.

Pinning up maps now, pinning my attention,
I cannot hold whole countries in my mind,
nor recognise their borders.

These days I want to trace
the shape of every townland in this valley;
name families; count trees, walls, cattle, gable-ends,
smoke-soft and tender in the near blue distance.

The Young Woman Stands on the Edge of Her Life

1

Saying the words
mother, daughter, sister.
A trinity more dense
than *father, brother, son.*

Mother, the deep mud in the yard.
Daughter, a bowl,
a love-word, a receptacle.
Sister, stands beside me,
her sword drawn.

Where will I live?
Down here in the earth
with the women?
Or upon the hill where the dogs bay
and the men
feed watchfires?

The cleft stick jumps in my hand.
The path seeks
its own way.

2

Where they buried the rabbit they planted the hazel tree.
The earth dragged at the new roots
which parted the crumbling flesh as sweetly
as touch parts silk
soaked years in the sun.
It was all decided and accomplished
before she remembered that she had forgotten
to make her choice.

The Husband's Tale

What is a wife?
                 She sits in the car and waits
while he opens the gates, the roses on the wall
all blown in the rain which is fine and warm
and just greys the green of high summer
like the fine strands now muting her hair.
She will drive to the small country town
and park in the station yard
and stand at the grooved wooden window
and take the ticket and wait in the rain for the train
to Dublin, to the doctor. . . .
                     And he thinks
how frail she is in her beige mac
in the green stew of roses and rain and birdsong,
how tired and quiet before the journey.
And he, in his strength, falters.
                     A loved wife is an underbelly
as soft and as stretched for the knife
as a frog's.

These Daily Dramas of Emigration

The slowing thump of the train –
three sisters on the platform,
their heads stamped
on the cruel green coin of the spring fields,
one with a travelling bag
and short aubergine-dyed hair,
black trousers, black boots, black
jacket, a clean face broken open,
closed shut again,
not so young anymore,
going again anyway,
and we could see at a thrown glance
she was not going to make it.

With our eyes practised on emigration
we could see more than that. We could see
how she must have made them suffer,
especially when the first husband
was brought home
and settled for.

The two of them walking
beside the train as it moves away,
waving, holding tight to
the stretch-armed child strung between them,
their long, undressed, mouse-gold hair caught
at the nape of each neck,
the older fatter
and in some sort of anonymous skirt,
the younger thinner
and in jeans,
their eyes anxious
and righteous,
not wanting her gone,
wanting her gone
and behaving badly somewhere else,
and everyone down the whole length of the train knowing
that when it has left they will turn their faces
back to the greening fields
and attend to their lives again.

All Night I Coughed

Sometimes
I stood wait by the window,
watching the shine
of the lambing lights
in the valley. Sometimes

I boiled kettles – potions
mulled from herbs.
Sometimes out there,
the book open in my lap,
earth and sand falling out of it,

brown bits of twigs
sliding after them,
discoloured flower-heads
buckling the pages, the names
yielded themselves:

Skullcap, angelica,
mullein, red clover,
horehound, borage.
Sickness:
its ancient practice.

And all the time
the flared blackness
of pneumonia's bombed dreams,
the farm lights, the fever,
the solitary watch –

and in the morning, in the light,
I was fish,
intent,
swimming my way through darkness
towards night.

Ship of Death

for my mother

Watching you, for the first time,
turn to prepare your boat, my mother;
making it clear you have other business now –
the business of your future –
I was washed-through with anger.

It was a first survey,
an eye thrown
over sails, oars, timbers,
as many a time I'd seen that practised eye
scan a laden table.

How can you plan going off like this
when we stand at last, close enough, if the wind is right,
to hear what the other is saying?
I never thought you'd do this, turning away,
mid-sentence, your hand testing a rope,

your ear tuned
to the small thunder of the curling wave
on the edge of the great-night sea,
neither regretful nor afraid –
anxious only for the tide.

Sick, Away from Home

for Jean Valentine

1

In the first flat I lay in bed, watched
the plane trees, their slow leaf-drift, the screen thinning.

In Ireland it was harvest still, the trees solid with leaves,
but a dry rattle, morning and night, when the winds blew.

2

This flat: roof-windows onto the sky;
the press of its pale eye against the glass.

3

A woman's voice in the room beside me.
Restrained, well-bred,
she speaks of the laying of carpets.
Footsteps. The scrape of a drawer.
I see her, thin and fairish, in her middle thirties.
I lie here, listening for her,
but she does not come again.
A tap runs where my left hand rests.
A man says he will feed the vine.

Her voice being as it was, I put on make-up when I get up.
Half-moons on their backs below my eyes.

4

Wakeful in the very early mornings
I let the walls form themselves
in blocks and planes. There is no such colour
as white. Sometimes rain falls on the sky-windows.
Sometimes birds' wings and the flighting of pigeons.

You can twist the blinds,
make them roof or sky.
The chancey sunlight sifts through slats,
corrugates the wall with stripes.

Secret days. Unknown to anyone.

5

I can feel the ground going
from under my feet.

This is a place
for the fairy-tale rule of three.
The bad bits
blacken before redemption.

And everywhere – on white sills, ledges, shelves –
a film of dust, laid down by the fall of air.

The Return

for Fiona Brooks Ward

When I came back alone to the house
it wasn't the same.
Not only the birds
that I nudged off paths,
or the flowers that stood
privately giving birth to themselves,

it was something more,
something to do with
its not being separate from itself;
not being the object
of anybody's care or scrutiny,
nor sheltering anyone.

It just *was*. Like an old house,
fallen in. Attentive. Still.
Lilac growing over the empty doorway.
Blackthorn at the gable end –
its fruiting of blue-black sloes,
the dense air caught on its thorns.

And I thought, is that what we are like?
Our own selves,

unregarded?
Do we stand somewhere,
as secret, sufficient, fierce?
And burdened with fragrance, like lilac?

A Childless Woman

With young women I am motherly,
With older women, daughterly,
With women of my own age, lonely.

1

First a landscape smudged with sound
and trickles of sound.
Air threaded with rain.

Where the swollen river has loosed its brown waters
into the marsh-places
and the shine of the cold sky shows in flatness of flood –
there the frogs grunt,

heave, flop about in watery eruptions,
stilling when they hear us,
but for an old bull, quivering, out of his head with sex,
who regards us balefully from his station
on a female, submerged
in the spawny glub and not protesting.

It is all woven – woods, sounds, light;
before the frills and flutterings begin.

2

I have a part-time, not-mine, son,
loaned from a woman that I never meet.

Sometimes I wonder if she thinks of me.

3
It's no big deal, happens over and over.
Just haunted, in spring, by the slow file
of the grey women who have made me.
And I am them, and I am breaking the line.
This is what it means: the year the spring didn't come.
Spilled water, seeping underground.

A fragile time, February going into March.

4
I am become a woman standing on the sidelines,
on station platforms meeting and seeing off trains,
casually surprised to be remembering
with gifts the anniversaries of friends' children.
A woman given
to speaking carefully, saying mostly the generous thing,
watching the brown flow of rivers,
waiting by windows open to the dusk.

Red Houses

for Frances

There are in this country, off small roads in darkness,
certain red houses.
Not the red of blood but the red of fire:
red from the red women who live in them.

I have been in one such house.
There was nothing special, nothing to show.
The wooden gates stood open, the dogs were in,
and on the raw concrete steps a bicycle

sprawled on its side in the thick black night air
that laid its wet finger to my face. Inside
the dark-haired red woman-of-the-house
stood by the table, pulled all eyes to her, and it was not

what she said, or did, or looked like, but the place
she drew her life from (some old ferned well
whose whereabouts I did not know) which so tuned her
that she glowed the house.

Fear for the children of such women,
especially the sons. For if they miss
the moment when it might be possible
to make the thing over again

they will spend their lives searching
through people and countries
and nowhere will they find again the red house
with the red heart in the soft black rainy night.

Interlude

for my father

My father told me how he dug up war graves,
picking out thigh bones – two per person – more accurate
than skulls which got mislaid and dumped.

I live in a house in a space in the fields.
This time of year we wake to swallows winging round the
bedroom;
earwigs and woodlice garrison dropped clothes,
mice quarry soap, harvest-spiders occupy all ceilings.

The house is quietly invaded. He puts down peas and beans;
I watch the fragile blossom of the cherry trees,
the distances smudge-blue, the mountains floating.
Sniff the green rain, mourn every passing,
greet each shoot until they are so crowded and so many
I cease recording and admit the summer.

Lives. Theirs, ours. Human times are mostly hard.
They will be so again. Some veil, insubstantial
as wound-gauze, separates this from that.

271

Notes to the Text

These notes explain mainly those words, expressions, and references that would be known by the literate Irish but not, perhaps, American reader, but also very arcane allusions which might thwart many readers, regardless of background. The notes neither intrude on a poem's deliberate secrecy nor offer information available in a good dictionary or basic reference book. Our guide to Hiberno-English expressions has been Terence Dolan's essential and recently published, *Dictionary of Hiberno-English* (Dublin: Gill and Macmillan, 1998). The poems of Ní Chuilleanáin and Ní Dhomhnaill require fuller notes, the first because she uses esoteric Catholic references, the second because her poetry draws heavily on traditional Irish culture.

Eavan Boland

PAGE 17: "Fond Memory"

the King had died: English monarch, George VI, who died in 1953. Boland's father was an Irish diplomat; hence the family lived a great deal out of Ireland. Boland spent her childhood first in London, then in New York.

the slow / lilts of Tom Moore: Thomas Moore (1779–1852), the son of a grocer, a graduate of Trinity College, Dublin. Moore knew well the patriot Robert Emmet but eschewed personal involvement with the revolutionary United Irishmen. Moore moved to England in 1800, stayed there for life, and became the darling of the London drawing room scene by performing his *Irish Melodies*, popular and sentimental songs about Ireland.

PAGE 20: "Achill Woman"

Achill: A desolate and dramatically beautiful island off the coast of Co. Mayo in the northwest corner of Ireland. This entire area, the province of Connaught, suffered more than any other part of Ireland during the Great Famine.

Court Poets of the Silver Age: presumably the title of an anthology of Elizabethan poetry.

PAGE 23: "That the Science of Cartography is Limited"

Relief Committees: Set up by an English Act of Parliament in 1847 to alleviate consequences of the Famine and comprised of English magistrates, Protestant and Catholic clergy, and large ratepayers, i.e. landlords. The committees are now regarded as having been neither successful nor remotely sufficient; hence the phrase has become a term of derision.

PAGE 24: "The Dolls Museum in Dublin"

The Green: Stephen's Green, where some of the action of the Easter 1916 rebellion took place, with troops of the Citizens' Army inside the iron-railings of the gracious, city-center park and in the College of Surgeons just outside the Green on the western side of the square. English troops occupied the posh, still standing Shelbourne Hotel, an icon of the Anglo-Irish Ascendancy, on the northern side of the square.

PAGE 31: "Anna Liffey"

Life: According to Norse mythology (and the Vikings did found Dublin), Life is like Eve, the mother of all things living. The myth affords Life, however, unlike Eve, autonomy and superiority over her quite subordinate consort who merely inseminates the life which Life, as it were, produces.

Eiléan Ní Chuilleanáin

PAGE 48: "Lucina Schynning in the Silence of the Nicht"

Title taken from the first line of the poem "The Birth of Antichrist," by William Dunbar (c. 1460–1525).

PAGE 49: "Now"

Maurice Craig: Born in 1919, published very formal, highly controlled poetry in the 1940's. His best-known work is a scholarly tome, *Dublin, 1660–1860,* a social and intellectual history of the city. Craig lives in Sandymount and often is visible working in the front room of his modest, Victorian terrace house on the Strand Road where the poet walks.

PAGE 53: "A Midwinter Prayer"

Samhain: Pronounced *sou·n*. An ancient Celtic festival (November 1), marking the beginning of winter.

Fionn: A hero of Irish mythology, specifically stories from the Fenian Cycle as distinct from the Ulster cycle, which features Cuchulainn as its hero. Fionn, a mortal descended from gods, was the leader of a band of men, the *fianna*, who lived on the margins of society, in the woods and fields. The *fianna*, from which the political term "Fenianism" derives, constituted a mobile army always ready for battle.

Plenary Indulgence: A term within Roman Catholic doctrine that refers to the remission of temporal punishment for sin. A plenary indulgence as distinct from a partial indulgence removes the entire debt.

Fenian men: Followers of Fionn, i.e. the *fianna*.

Munster: One of the four provinces of Ireland: Leinster, Munster, Ulster, and Connaght. Munster is in the southern quadrant.

PAGE 63: "J'ai Mal à nos Dents"

The title translates from the French as "I have a pain in our teeth."

J'étais à moité saoûle: "I was half drunk."

J'ai mangerai les pissenlits par les racines: A French expression that translates as "I will be pushing up daisies."

Une malade à soigner une malade: "The sick looking after the sick."

PAGE 64: "St Mary Magdalene Preaching at Marseilles"

According to popular tradition, Mary Magdalene was a former prostitute who became a follower of Christ. She ministered to him in Galilee and later stood at the foot of the cross at the Crucifixion. She was also present at the discovery of Christ's open tomb, and witnessed an appearance of the risen Christ on the same day. Legend has it that after Christ's death, she and Martha and Lazarus traveled to the south of France by sea. Also according to legend, Mary Magdalene became a preacher in Marseilles after the death of Christ.

PAGE 65: "'He Hangs in Shades the Orange Bright'"

Title taken from Andrew Marvel's "Bermudas." Lines 17 and 18 of that poem read: "He hangs in shades the orange bright, / Like golden lamps in a green night."

PAGE 70: "The Real Thing"

the Brazen Serpent: A complex, even paradoxical, symbol. According to the Bible, it was an artifact with supposed healing properties constructed by Moses in the wilderness for the benefit of the Israelites, who earlier had been attacked by deadly serpents. (Num. 21, 4–9 and John 3, 14–15.)

PAGE 71: "Saint Margaret of Cortona"

Margaret of Cortona (1249–97) was born in Laviano, Tuscany, and died in Cortona. After living for some time as a concubine, she repented and entered a Franciscan convent. Church tradition has it that she became a model of penitence and charity.

PAGE 75: "Vierge Ouvrante"

French term for a small statue of the Virgin Mary that is constructed to open to reveal the Virgin's heart.

PAGE 82: "Translation (for the reburial of the Magdalens)"

Magdalens: Women who have borne a child out of wedlock and who have been consigned to communities that seek to reform these women. Some Magdalens spent their entire lives virtually imprisoned in these communities, usually working as laundresses. The poem refers specifically to a re-interment ceremony in the early 1990's of Irish women who had served in a Magdalen laundry earlier in the century. The reburial took place when the convent lands were sold and the remains removed to Glasnevin Cemetery without the knowledge or consent of the women's families.

PAGE 83: "Alcove"

Paolo and Francesca: Francesca was the daughter of a lord of Ravenna. She was married to Malatesta, a lord of Rimini, but loved his brother, Paolo. Her husband discovered their passion and murdered them around 1289. In Dante's *Divine Comedy* (*Inferno*, Canto Five), she appears with Paolo in circle two of Hell,

276

where sins involved with carnal love are punished. She tells her own story in Dante.

Medbh McGuckian

PAGE 105: "Gigot Sleeves"

Shane Murphy in his article "Obliquity in the Poetry of Paul Muldoon and Medbh McGuckian" (see bibliography) convincingly argues that the provenance of this poem about Emily Bronte is McGuckian's reading of the biography of the Victorian novelist by Winfred Gérin, *Emily Bronte: A Biography* (Oxford: OUP, 1978).

Trelawney: Edward John Trelawney (1792–1881), an English writer and adventurer who became friendly in Italy in 1822 with Shelley and Byron. Trelawney, who was acutely grief-stricken by Shelley's death by drowning, arranged to have his own ashes buried next to the Romantic poet's in Rome. Trelawney wrote *Records of Shelley, Byron and the Author* (1878).

PAGE 120: "The Albert Chain"

The title refers to a popular necklace.

PAGE 122: "Pulsus Paradoxus"

The title refers to an arrhythmic condition of the heart.

PAGE 122: "Shelmalier"

The title refers to a distinct people in Wexford, the *siol malure,* who were wiped out in a series of English offensives. When the English later mapped the area, the name became anglicized into Shelmalier, referring to a Barony in Wexford. The name appears in two famous nineteenth-century ballads that commemorate the rebellion of 1798. One is a song that praises the efforts of Father John Murphy, a patriot priest, and names Shelmalier as the location in Wexford where the rebels assembled. The other is a traditional ballad, "Kelly the Boy from Killane," which begins: "What's the news, what's the news, O my bold Shelmalier?" Shelmalier has become a synonym for a participant in the 1798 rebellion. These poems interweave information and lore from the 1798 rebellion and from the Troubles in the North, as well as personal experiences and reflections.

Nuala Ní Dhomhnaill

PAGE 130: "Cú Chullain II"

Cuchullain is the great hero of the Ulster Cycle of mythology, the *Táin Bó Cuailnge* (The Cattle Raid of Cooley) being its most famous text. In this epic saga, Cuchullain is the great protector of Ulster. A formidable warrior, Cuchullain is notorious for the paranormal, physical transformations, in fact bodily distortions, he underwent in battle. Ní Dhomhnaill's poem addresses special mysteries and sadnesses attached to Cuchullain's paternal lineage, specifically that the identity of his own father is obscure, even incest being suggested, and that, later in his life, not recognizing his own son, Cuchullain killed the young man in battle.

St John's Eve: The evening before St. John the Baptist's Day, Midsummer Eve. Ní Dhomhnaill adds ". . . the start of the Lughnasa Festival and even during my childhood in every townland in West Kerry, huge bonfires used to be made, and cattle driven between them, and couples used to jump over them for good luck. Liam Ó Muirthile has a long dramatic poem on the subject called *"Tine Chnamh."*

PAGE 136: "The Head"

joiner: Carpenter.

Belt: Physical blow.

Deal: Pine.

1784 . . . the Year of the Bad Spring: Ní Dhomhnaill explains, "The Year of the Bad Spring was an earlier Famine year, as far as I remember 1780 or thereabouts. It was earlier than the year of *'La Maraithe na bhFear sa Daingean,'* the 'Massacre in Dingle,' which was 1794, when the Kerry Militia under the command of the brother of Lord Ventry fired on a rioting crowd on Main Street in Dingle and left thirty dead."

He oxters Tommy up: Hiberno-English, to lift by the underarms, the oxters.

PAGE 140: "Miraculous Grass"

my green, unfortunate field: Reference to Ireland under domination, usually made by a symbolic, visionary woman who personifies the nation, alias Kathleen Ní Houlihan.

PAGE 142: "As for the Quince"

lost the rag: Hiberno-English, lost one's temper.

Ladyship: Term of mild derision of a female child or woman who puts on airs.

PAGE 146: "As Fragile as a Shell"

the Angelus: A devotional exercise commemorating the Incarnation, said by Roman Catholics at morning, noon, and sunset, at the sound of a bell. This is a very audible ritual in the Republic of Ireland, inasmuch as the national broadcasting company, RTÉ (*Radio Telefís Éireann*), interrupts programming at 6 p.m. to ring the angelus.

PAGE 150: "Nude"

oxter: See note for "The Head."

PAGE 152–153: "Hag"

cailleach: Irish for a hag, a very old woman, and a conventional trope in traditional Irish poetry and story.

Fenian tales: See above, Ní Chuilleanáin's "Midsummer Eve," the reference to Fionn.

PAGE 159: "Carnival"

Part 1 *dark passageway:* A reference to the souterain, or long passageway, of a pre-Christian burial mound, which at Newgrange in County Louth is engineered to receive in its inner chamber the first rays of the sun at the summer solstice.

Part 3 *you Sualtam or the Daghda:* Ní Dhomhnaill explains, "The myth is that the god Sualtam slept with the river-goddess of the Boyne and the child resulting from this was Aongus. So that her husband Neachtain wouldn't notice anything amiss, Sualtam caused the sun to stay in the sky for a whole year, so that Boann could be pregnant with Aongus and give birth to him without her husband noticing. In some versions of the myth it is Daghda, the father of the Celtic gods, who sleeps with her, and so Aongus is often called Aongus Og (i.e., young) Mac an Daghda."

PAGE 163: "The Battering"

fairy fort: A round barrow, an ancient burial site. Legend has it this is where the "other" or fairy people live.

Sudocrem: An all-purpose white, zinc ointment in Ireland, a miracle cure, especially effective with "nappy" (diaper) rash.

sign of the cross with the tongs: The fairies could not tolerate, therefore were exorcised by, iron.

PAGE 166: "First Communion"

the woman in the road who vexes / over her gaggle of geese: Ní Dhomhnaill reports, "This is a line lifted straight out of the Jacobite song *"Sean O Duibhir an Ghleanna"* ("John O'Dwyer of the Glen"), who was one of the last of the Rapparees, or those soldiers who held out against going abroad after the Siege of Limerick. It is really an image of Ireland crying over the scattering of the Wild Geese," Irish aristocracy who fled to the continent after defeat at the Battle of Kinsale in 1601.

PAGE 168: "Deep Freeze"

healing well: Peter Harbison in *Pilgrimage in Ireland* (London: Barrie & Jenkins, 1991), pp. 229–234, observes of "healing" or "holy wells" that these pilgrimage sites were local rather than national in character. He says, "Even in the nineteenth century, few wells would have attracted visitors from a distance of more than about twenty miles around; this is understandable when we realize that there were anything up to 3,000 such wells in Ireland. Many visits were undertaken not solely to perform religious exercises and duties; they were festive social occasions where people from surrounding areas could meet to exchange views and settle personal matters once a year on the local saint's feast day."

Jimin Mhaire Thaidhg: Ní Dhomhnaill explains, "Jimin Mhaire Thaidhg is a character in a story for children in Irish who is the equivalent of Dennis the Menace. At one point he and his friend, Micilin Eoin, drown the family cat, purely in the spirit of experiment, just to see is it really true that a cat has nine lives. The cat comes back to haunt him again and again, and that is what it is doing in my deep-freeze, haunting me as well. And yes, the ditch or long barrow can be construed as famine graves. A bit like the pit in Paul [Muldoon]'s 'Cauliflowers'."

PAGE 170: "Cathleen"

Ní Dhomhnaill glosses many references in this densely inter-
textual poem: "Many descriptions of the Aisling / Ireland
woman, describe her as swan-like. I think I was thinking in
particular of the song 'The Coolen' / 'An Chuilfhionn.' Also
there is a line in that song that translates roughly as "and your
man Power who was the captain of the ship / said he would
prefer to have her for himself than Ireland undivided."
(Because of course She is Ireland.)

Black and Tan Bottom: The Black and Tans were infamous, special
British troops deployed during the Anglo-Irish War with a
particular reputation for brutality. The name derives from the
fact that this police force, largely consisting of ex-soldiers from
Britain, was so hastily assembled that they had no proper
uniforms and wore khaki with police caps and belts. The Black
Bottom was a dance of the 1920's.

beauties most beautied . . . brightest of bright: A reference to Aogán Ó
Rathaille's (c. 1675–1729) most famous aisling, the poem "Gile
na Gile," translated by Thomas Kinsella as "Brightness Most
Bright." The first stanza introduces the vision of Ireland as a
beautiful woman: "Brightness most bright, I beheld on the
way, forlorn. / Crystal of crystal her eye, blue touched with
green. / Sweetness most sweet her voice, not stern with age. /
Colour and pallor appeared in her flushed cheek."

dream vision: An aisling.

red rose, proud: A reference to poems from Yeats's 1893 volume,
The Rose; e.g. "The Rose Upon the Rood of Time," which
ends ". . . I would, before my time to go / Sing of old Eire and
the ancient ways / Red Rose, proud Rose, sad Rose of all my
days."

Rita Ann Higgins

PAGE 187: "Consumptive in the Library"

Sweet Afton: A brand of Irish cigarettes.

PAGE 189: "It's All Because We're Working Class"

coal bag washer: a compulsively tidy person.

PAGE 190: "She is Not Afraid of Burglars"

Eyre Square: at the center of Galway City, the major meeting place.

PAGE 194: "Be Someone"

Humber Scepter: A mid-sized automobile.

PAGE 200: "Some People"

the Vincent de Paul: A Catholic charity.

blanket man: A collector of payments on goods bought on the installment plan.

PAGE 201: "Philomena's Revenge"

Philomena: A former saint whose cult, authorized by Pope Gregory XVI in 1837, originated with the discovery of the skeleton of a young girl and a small vial with a residue believed to be blood in a catacomb in Rome in 1802. An inscription near the tomb read: "Peace be with thee, Philomena." In 1961, however, because veneration of her was said to be based on fervor rather than fact, the Church removed her name from the calendar of saints.

craic: Originally British "crack," a term recycled in Irish, meaning lively conversation and other fun.

PAGE 205: "Old Timers"

clockman: A child's name for a municipal night watchman.

Jeyes Fluid: A ubiquitous, cheap cleaning agent with an insidious odor.

PAGE 208: "Remapping the Borders"

Siege of Ennis: An Irish traditional dance set.

Paula Meehan

PAGE 214: "Zugzwang"

A dead-end situation in chess.

PAGE 217: "The Pattern"

flat: apartment

282

PAGE 220: "Child Burial"

gansy: Hiberno-English for a knitted jersey or wool sweater, not a cardigan, a pullover.

PAGE 225: "My Love about His Business in the Barn"

hoke: to rummage or poke through assorted, random things.

dodgy: evasive, tricky, artful

mooching: idling in a suspicious manner, loafing about, being on the lookout for picking up something for nothing.

gasometer: large reservoir in which gas is stored for distribution by pipes.

Moya Cannon

PAGE 234: "Crannóg"

The title is Irish for a prehistoric lake-dwelling, an artificially created island in a lake, an example of which is Loch Gur in County Limerick. Crannógs were used as places of defensive residence during the Iron Age.

PAGE 238: "Scríob"

The title is Irish for a scratch, a scraping, a scoring, a mark in a field to guide the ploughman.

Mary O'Malley

PAGE 245: "Cornered"

gaffed: Presumably impaled on the question, because a gaff is a barbed fishing spear, or large hook to haul in fish.

PAGE 247: "The Cave"

The grey ancestors of the Mac Conghaile: The Mac Conghailes, among other families were, according to legend, descended from the selkies, the seal women.

PAGE 249: "Cealtrach"

Even into this century, the place where unbaptized babies and still-borns were buried, since the Church wouldn't allow them

283

to be buried in consecrated ground. Often the cealtrach was located where an early Christian settlement used to be; hence, the ground resonated with another kind of sanctity, one not recognized by the Church.

unchurched: refers to churching, "a form of thanksgiving formerly made by Christian women after childbirth, involving the woman kneeling at the back of the church holding a lighted candle. She would be sprinkled with holy water by the priest, who would recite Psalm 23 and then lead her to the altar-rails, where certain prayers and responses were said, followed by a prayer for the well-being of the mother and child and a final blessing (mothers were recommended, but not bound, to receive it)" (Dolan). The common feminist interpretation of the practice is that it is a purification rite, as evidenced by the advancement of the just-delivered mother from the back of the church to the front, after the administering of holy water.

PAGE 251: "Liadan with a Mortgage Briefly Tastes the Stars"

Liadan: A poetess with whom the poet Cuirthir fell in love. Theirs is a sorrowful tale of thwarted love, not unlike that of Heloise and Abelard. Instead of waiting for Cuirthir to marry her, Liadan became a nun. In despair, Cuirthir took holy orders and entered a monastery. They both regretted and suffered from their actions. Cuirthir was eventually exiled from Ireland and Liadan lay down on his grave and, uttering a powerful lament, died of grief.

Croagh Patrick: or Patrick's Mountain, in Co. Mayo, associated with St Patrick where an annual pilgrimage takes place. Tradition has it that St Patrick went up the mountain to fast and pray, like Moses, for forty days and forty nights. Every summer pilgrims re-enact the ascent, often barefoot, as a penitential exercise.

stravaiging: to wander aimlessly.

PAGE 252: "The Maighdean Mhara"

Maighdean Mhara is the usual Irish for a mermaid. It translates literally as Sea Virgin. Interestingly, Ní Dhomhnaill in her mermaid poems uses the word "muruach," which is genderless.

284

PAGE 252: "Gráinne's Answer to Burke's Proposal"

The Gráinne referred to here is not the Gráinne of mythology, but the Gráinne of popular legend and history, e.g. Grainnuaile, Grace O'Malley, the famous female pirate from Mayo who lived in the 1600's on Clare Island off the coast. The Burkes were a major landholding family in Mayo.

Biographical Notes

Eavan Boland was born in Dublin in 1944. The daughter of an Irish diplomat and the painter, Frances Kelly, Boland spent much of her childhood in London and New York. She is a graduate of Trinity College, Dublin, and one of the founders of the Irish feminist publishing company, Arlen House. Her husband is the novelist, Kevin Casey, and they have two grown daughters. Boland now divides her time between Dublin and California, where she is the Director of the Creative Writing Program at Stanford University. She has been the recipient of many awards, among them a Lannan Foundation Award in Poetry and an American Ireland Fund Literary Award.

Eiléan Ní Chuilleanáin was born in Cork in 1942. The daughter of a Professor of Irish and the novelist, Eilís Dillon, Ní Chuilleanáin was educated at University College, Cork, and Oxford University. She lives in Dublin, and lectures at Trinity College, Dublin, in Medieval and Renaissance Literature. Currently she is the chairman of the English Department. With her husband, MacDara Woods, and three other poets, she edits the literary magazine, *Cyphers*. She is the mother of one son. Among other honors, she has won the *Irish Times* Award for Poetry, the Patrick Kavanagh Award, and the O'Shaughnessy Award from the Irish-American Cultural Institute.

Medbh McGuckian was born in 1950 in Belfast, where she still lives with her husband and four children. McGuckian, who once taught school, was the first woman to be appointed Writer-in-Residence at Queens University, her alma mater. She has also been a Visiting Fellow at the University of California, Berkeley. She has been the recipient of many awards, including the Alice Hunt Bartlett Prize, the Cheltenham Award, and the Bass Ireland Award. She also has won Britain's National Poetry Competition.

Nuala Ní Dhomhnaill was born in England in 1952, the daughter of two Irish doctors. She spent much of her childhood in the Irish-speaking areas of West Kerry and Tipperary. She studied at University College, Cork, and now lives in Dublin. She has spent several years in Turkey and still returns there regularly with her Turkish husband and four children. Ní Dhomhnaill has held the Burns Chair of Irish Studies at Boston College and is the contemporary poetry editor of the forthcoming fourth volume of the *Field Day Anthology of Irish Writing*. All four of her collections of poems in Irish have won the Seán Ó Ríordáin Award. She received the Arts Council Prize for Poetry on three occasions and the Butler Award from the Irish American Cultural Institution.

Rita Ann Higgins was born in Galway in 1955, one of eleven children. She left school when she was fourteen and began writing poetry in her twenties. She has been a Writer-in-Residence at University College, Galway, and has conducted a series of poetry workshops in prisons in Ireland and England. *Sunny Side Plucked: New and Selected Poems* was awarded the English Poetry Book Society Recommendation in 1996. She is also the author of three plays, two of which have been staged by the Punchbag Theatre Company in Galway. She has been the recipient of many awards for her work, including the Peadear O'Donnell Award and the *Irish Times* / Aer Lingus Literary Award.

Paula Meehan was born in 1955 in Dublin, where she now lives. She studied at Trinity College, Dublin, and at Eastern Washington University in the United States. She has received a number of awards for her work including the Marten Toonder Award for Literature and The Butler Award for Poetry from the Irish American Cultural Institute. She is also the author of two plays.

Moya Cannon was born in Donegal in 1956. A graduate of both University College, Dublin, and Corpus Christi College, Cambridge, she now lives in Galway, where she teaches in a school for adolescent travelers. She has been Writer-in-Residence at Trent University, Ontario, and editor of *Poetry Ireland Review*. In 1990, she won the Brendan Behan Award for the best first collection of poetry.

Mary O'Malley was born in Connemara in 1954. She graduated from University College, Galway, and taught at the New University of Lisbon in Portugal for eight years. A recipient of the Hennessey Award in 1990, she contributes regularly to Irish television and radio. As a result of a long association with Inish Mor, the largest of the Aran Islands, she helped form a writing group there. She now lives in the Moycullen *Gaeltacht* with her husband and two children.

Kerry Hardie was born in 1951 in Singapore and grew up in Co. Down in Northern Ireland. She now lives in Co. Kilkenny with her husband, the novelist, Seán Hardie. The winner of a number of prizes, including the Bournemouth International Festival prize in 1995, she was a joint winner of the Hennessey Award in 1995. A second collection of poems and a novel entitled *Hannie Bennett* are both forthcoming.

Selected Bibliography

Eavan Boland

VOLUMES OF POETRY

New Territory. Dublin: Allen, Figgis & Co., 1967.

The War Horse. Dublin: Arlen House; London: Victor Gollancz, 1975.

In Her Own Image. Dublin: Arlen House, 1980.

Introducing Eavan Boland: Poems. Princeton: The Ontario Review Press, 1981.

Night Feed. Dublin: Arlen House; London and Boston: Marion Boyars, 1982; Manchester: Carcanet Press, 1994.

The Journey and Other Poems. Dublin: Arlen House, 1986; Manchester: Carcanet, 1987.

Selected Poems. Manchester: Carcanet Press; Dublin: Arlen House, 1989.

Outside History. Manchester: Carcanet Press, 1990.

Outside History: Selected Poems 1980-1990. New York: Norton, 1990.

In a Time of Violence. Manchester: Carcanet; New York: Norton, 1994.

An Origin Like Water: Collected Poems 1967-1987. New York and London: Norton, 1997.

The Lost Land. New York and London: Norton, 1998.

OTHER WORKS BY BOLAND

"The Woman Poet: Her Dilemma." *Midland Review* 3 (1986): 40–47. Also in *Krino* (Spring, 1986); *Stand Magazine* (Winter 1986–87): 43–49; and *American Poetry Review* 16:1 (Jan./Feb. 1987): 17–20.

"An Un-Romantic American." *Parnassus: Poetry in Review* 14, no. 2 (1988): 73–92.

"The Woman Poet in a National Tradition." *Studies* 76: 148–158. Also published as "A Kind of Scar: The Woman Poet in a National Tradition." Dublin: Attic LIP Pamphlet, 1989.

"Outside History." *American Poetry Review* 19.2 (March/April 1990): 32–38.

"The Woman, The Place, The Poet." *Georgia Review* 44, 1–2 (1990): 97–109.

"In Defense of Workshops." *Poetry Ireland Review* 31 (1991): 40–48.

"Writing in the Margin." *Irish Times* (April 18, 1992): 12.

291

Object Lessons: The Life of the Woman and the Poet in Our Time. New York and London: Norton, 1995.

"Writing the Political Poem in Ireland." *The Southern Review* (July 1995): 485–498.

"New Wave 2: Born in the '50's; Irish Poets of the Global Village." *Irish Poets since Kavanagh.* Edited by Theo Dorgan. Blackrock, Co. Dublin: Four Courts Press, 1996.

"Daughters of Colony." *Eire-Ireland,* 32, 2 & 3 (1997): 7–20.

INTERVIEWS

Consalvo, Deborah McWilliams. "An Interview with Eavan Boland." *Studies: An Irish Quarterly Review* 181: 321 (Spring 1992): 89–100.

O'Connell, Patty. "Eavan Boland: An Interview." *Poets & Writers* (November–December 1994): 32–45.

Reizbaum, Marilyn. "An Interview with Eavan Boland." *Contemporary Literature* 30, no. 4 (1989): 470–490.

Tall, Deborah. "Q&A with Eavan Boland." *Irish Literary Supplement* 7, no. 2 (1988): 39–40.

Wright, Nancy Means and Dennis Hannan. "Q&A with Eavan Boland." *Irish Literary Supplement* (Spring 1991): 10–11.

CRITICISM ON BOLAND

Allen-Randolphe, Jody. "Ecriture Feminine and the Authorship of Self in Eavan Boland's *In Her Own Image.*" *Colby Quarterly* 27, 1 (March 1991): 48–59.

———. "Private Worlds, Public Realities: Eavan Boland's Poetry, 1967–1990." *Irish University Review* 23,1 (1993): 5–22.

———. "Finding a Voice where She Found a Vision." *PN Review* 2, 1 (September–October 1994): 13–17.

——— and Anthony Roche. "Eavan Boland–Special Issue." *Irish University Review* 23, 1 (1993).

Atfield, Rose. "Postcolonialism in the Poetry and Essays of Eavan Boland." *A Cultural Review* 8, 2 (Spring 1997): 168–182.

Brown, Susan. "A Victorian Sappho: Agency, Identity and the Politics of Poetics." *ESC* 20, 2 (June 1994): 205–225.

Cannon, M. Louise. "The Extraordinary Within the Ordinary: The Poetry of Eavan Boland and Nuala Ní Dhomhnaill.' *South Atlantic Review* 60: 2: 31–46.

Conboy, Sheila C. "'What You Have Seen is Beyond Speech.' Female Journeys in the Poetry of Eavan Boland and Eiléan Ní Chuilleanáin." *Canadian Journal of Irish Studies* 16 (1990): 65–72.

———. "Eavan Boland's Topography of Displacement." *Eire-Ireland* 29, 3 (1994): 137–146.

Consalvo, Deborah. "In Common Usage: Eavan Boland's Poetic Voice." *Eire-Ireland* 28 (Summer 1993): 100–115.

Denman, Peter. "Ways of Saying: Boland, Carson, McGuckian." *Poetry in Contemporary Irish Literature.* Edited by Michael Kenneally, pp. 158–73. Gerrard's Cross: Colin Smythe, 1995.

Haberstroh, Patricia Boyle. "Eavan Boland." *Women Creating Women,* pp. 59–90. Syracuse: Syracuse University Press, 1996.

———. "Woman, Artist and Image in *Night Feed.*" *Irish University Review* 23, 1 (1993): 67–94.

Hagen, Patricia L. and Thomas W. Zelman. "'We Were Never on the Scene of the Crime': Eavan Boland's Repossession of History." *Twentieth Century Literature* 37, 4 (Winter 1991): 442–452.

Heuving, Jeanne. "Poetry in Our Political Lives." *Contemporary Literature* 37, 2 (1996): 315–332.

Kelly, Sylvia. "The Silent Cage and Female Creativity in *In Her Own Image.*" *Irish University Review* 23, 1 (1993): 45–56.

Luftig, Victor. "'Something Will Happen to You Who Read': Adrienne Rich, Eavan Boland." *Irish University Review* 23, 1 (1993): 57–66.

Mahon, Derek. "Young Eavan and Early Boland." *Irish University Review* 23, 1 (1993): 23–8.

Mahon, Ellen M. "Eavan Boland's Journey with the Muse." *Learning the Trade: Essays on W.B. Yeats and Contemporary Poetry.* Edited by Deborah Fleming, pp. 179–194. West Cornwall, Ct: Locust Hill, 1993.

Paddon, Seija. "The Diversity of Performance / Performance as Diversity in the Poetry of Laura (Riding) Jackson and Eavan Boland." *ES Can* 22, 4 (1996): 425–439.

Raschke, Debra. " Eavan Boland's 'Outside History' and 'In a Time of Violence': Rescuing Women, the Concrete, and other Things Physical from the Dung Heap." *Colby Quarterly* 32, 2 (1996): 135–142.

Reizbaum, Marilyn. "What's My Line: the Contemporaneity of Eavan Boland." *Irish University Review* 23, 1 (1993): 100–10.

Sarbin, Deborah. "'Out of Myth into History': The Poetry of Eavan Boland and Eiléan Ní Chuilleanáin." *Canadian Journal of Irish Studies* 19, 1 (July 1993): 86–96.

Weekes, Ann Owens. "'An Origin like Water': The Poetry of Eavan Boland and Modernist Critiques of Irish Literature." *Bucknell Review* 38, 1 (1994): 159–76.

Eiléan Ní Chuilleanáin

VOLUMES OF POETRY

Acts and Monuments. Dublin: Gallery Press, 1972.

Site of Ambush. Dublin: Gallery, 1975.

The Second Voyage. Winston-Salem, NC: Wake Forest University Press; Dublin: Gallery Press, 1977. 2nd edition, Dublin: Gallery Press, 1986; Winston-Salem, NC: Wake Forest University Press, 1989.

Cork. Dublin: Gallery Press: 1977

The Rose Geranium. Dublin: Gallery Press, 1981.

The Magdalene Sermon. Oldcastle, Co. Meath: Gallery Press, 1989.

The Magdalene Sermon and Other Poems. Winston-Salem, NC: Wake Forest University Press, 1991

The Brazen Serpent. Oldcastle, Co. Meath: Gallery Press, 1994; Winston-Salem, N.C.: Wake Forest University Press, 1995.

OTHER WORKS BY NÍ CHUILLEANÁIN

"Woman as Writer: The Social Matrix." *Crane Bag* 4, 1, (1980): 101–105.

Introduction to *Irish Women: Image and Achievement*. Edited by Eiléan Ní Chuilleanáin, pp. 1–11. Dublin: Arlen House, 1985.

"Women As Writers: Dánta Grá to Maria Edgeworth." *Irish Women Image and Achievement*. Edited by Eiléan Ní Chuilleanáin, pp. 111–126. Dublin: Arlen House, 1985.

"Acts and Monuments of an Unelected Nation: The *Cailleach* Writes about the Renaissance." *The Southern Review* 31, 3 (July 1995): 570–80.

INTERVIEWS

Consalvo, Deborah McWilliams. "An Interview with Eiléan Ní Chuilleanáin." *Irish Literary Supplement* 12, 1 (1993): 15–17.

Ray, Kevin. "Interview with Eiléan Ní Chuilleanáin." *Eire-Ireland* 32, 1 & 2 (1996): 62–73.

CRITICISM ON NÍ CHUILLEANÁIN

Conboy, Sheila C. "'What You Have Seen is Beyond Speech.' Female Journeys in the Poetry of Eavan Boland and Eiléan Ní Chuilleanáin." *Canadian Journal of Irish Studies* 16 (1990): 65–72.

Foster, John Wilson. "'The Second Voyage' by Eiléan Ní Chuilleanáin." *Eire-Ireland* 13, 4 (1978): 147–51.

Grennan, Eamon. "Real Things." *Poetry Ireland Review* 46 (Summer 1995): 44–52.

Haberstroh, Patricia Boyle. "Eiléan Ní Chuilleanáin." *Women Creating Women*, pp. 93–120. Syracuse: Syracuse University Press, 1996.

Johnston, Dillon. "'Our Bodies' Eyes and Writing Hands': Secrecy and Sensuality in Ní Chuilleanáin's Baroque Art." *Gender and Sexuality in Modern Ireland*. Edited by Anthony Bradley and Maryann Gialanella Valiulis, pp. 187–211. Amherst: University of Massachusetts Press, 1997.

Kerrigan, John. "Hidden Ireland: Eiléan Ní Chuilleanáin and Munster Poetry." *Critical Quarterly* 40, No. 4 (Winter 1998): 76–100.

Meaney, Geraldine. "History Gasps: Myth in Contemporary Irish Women's Poetry." *Poetry in Contemporary Irish Literature*. Edited by Michael Kenneally, pp. 99–113. Gerrards Cross: Colin Smythe, 1995.

Sarbin, Deborah. "'Out of Myth into History': The Poetry of Eavan Boland and Eiléan Ní Chuilleanáin." *Canadian Journal of Irish Studies* 19, 1 (July 1993): 86–96.

Sirr, Peter. "'How Things Begin to Happen': Notes on Eiléan Ní Chuilleanáin and Medbh McGuckian." *The Southern Review* 31, 3 (Summer 1995). 450–467.

Medbh McGuckian

VOLUMES OF POETRY

Portrait of Joanna. Belfast: Ulsterman Publications, 1980.

Single Ladies. Budleigh Salterton: Interim, 1982.

The Flower Master. Oxford: Oxford University Press, 1982; Oldcastle, Co. Meath: Gallery Press, 1993.

Venus and the Rain. Oxford: Oxford University Press, 1984; Oldcastle, Co. Meath: Gallery Press, 1994.

On Ballycastle Beach. Oxford: Oxford University Press; Winston-Salem, N.C.; Wake Forest University Press, 1988; Oldcastle, Co. Meath: Gallery Press, 1995.

——— and Nuala Archer. *Two Women, Two Shores: Poems by Medbh McGuckian and Nuala Archer*. Baltimore, Md: New Poets Series, 1989.

Marconi's Cottage. Oldcastle, Co. Meath: Gallery Press; Winston - Salem, N.C.: Wake Forest University Press, 1991.

The Flower Master and Other Poems. Oldcastle, Co. Meath: Gallery Press, 1993.

Captain Lavender. Oldcastle, Co. Meath: Gallery Press; Winston-Salem, N.C.: Wake Forest University Press, 1995.

Selected Poems: 1978–1994. Oldcastle, Co. Meath: Gallery Press; Winston-Salem, N.C.: Wake Forest University Press, 1997.

Shelmalier. Oldcastle, Co. Meath: Gallery Press; Winston Salem, N.C.: Wake Forest University Press, 1999.

OTHER WORKS BY MCGUCKIAN

"Don't Talk to Me about Dance." *Poetry Ireland Review* 35, 1992: 98–100.

"Comhra, with a Foreward and Afterword by Laura O'Connor." *The Southern Review* 31, 3(Summer 1995): 581–614.

"Home." *Hope and History: Eyewitness Accounts of Life in Twentieth-Century Ulster*. Edited by Sophia H. King and Sean McMahon, pp. 210–211. Belfast: Friar's Bush Press, 1996.

INTERVIEWS

McGrath, Niall. "The McGuckian Enigma: Interview with Medbh McGuckian." *Causeway* (Summer 1994): 67–70.

Bohman, Kimberly S. "Surfacing: An Interview with Medbh McGuckian, Belfast, 5th September, 1994." *The Irish Review* 16 (Autumn/Winter 1994): 95–108.

Brandes, Rand. "A Dialogue with Medbh McGuckian." *Studies in the Literary Imagination* 30, 2 (1997): 37–61.

———. "An Interview with Medbh McGuckian." *The Chattahoochee Review* 16, 3, Spring 1996, pp. 56–65.

McCracken, Kathleen. "An Attitude of Compassion." *Irish Literary Supplement* 9, 2 (Fall 1990): 20–21.

Sailer, Susan Shaw. "An Interview with Medbh McGuckian." *Michigan Review*, 32, 1 (Winter 1993): 111–127.

CRITICISM ON MCGUCKIAN

Batten, Guinn. "'The More With Which We are Connected': The Muse of the Minus in the Poetry of McGuckian and Kinsella." *Gender and Sexuality in Modern Ireland*. Edited by Anthony Bradley and Maryann Gialanella Valiulis, pp. 212–244. Amherst: University of Massachusetts Press, 1997.

Beer, Ann. "Medbh McGuckian's Poetry: Maternal Thinking and a Politics of Peace." *Canadian Journal of Irish Studies* 18,1 (1992): 192–203.

Bendell, Molly. "Flower Logic: The Poems of Medbh McGuckian." *Antioch Review* 48, 3 (Summer 1990): 367–371.

296

Cahill, Eileen. "'Because I never garden': Medbh McGuckian's Solitary Way." *Irish University Review* 24, 2 (1994): 264–71.

Denman, Peter. "Ways of Saying: Boland, Carson, McGuckian." *Poetry in Contemporary Irish Literature.* Edited by Michael Kenneally, pp. 158–73. Gerrard's Cross: Colin Smythe, 1995.

Docherty, Thomas. "Initiations, Tempers, Seductions: Postmodern McGuckian." *The Chosen Ground: Essays on the Contemporary Poetry of Northern Ireland.* Edited by Neil Corcoran, pp. 191–212. Chester Springs, PA: Dufour Editions, 1992.

Grey, Cecile. "Medbh McGuckian: Imagery Wrought to its Uttermost." *Learning the Trade: Essays on W.B. Yeats and Contemporary Poetry.* Edited by Deborah Fleming, pp. 165–177. West Cornwall, CT: Locust Hill, 1993.

Haberstroh, Patricia Boyle. "Medbh McGuckian." *Women Creating Women,* pp. 123–158. Syracuse: Syracuse University Press, 1996.

Murphy, Shane. "Obliquity in the Poetry of Paul Muldoon and Medbh McGuckian." *Eire-Ireland* 31, 3 & 4 (1996): 76–101.

O'Brien, Peggy. "Reading Medbh McGuckian: Admiring What We Cannot Understand." *Colby Quarterly* 37, 4 (December 1992): 239–50.

O'Connor, Mary. "'Rising Out': Medbh McGuckian's Destabilizing Poetics." *Eire-Ireland* 30,4 (Winter 1996): 154–172.

Porter, Mary. "The Imaginative Space of Medbh McGuckian." *International Women's Writing: New Landscapes of Identity.* Edited by Anne Brown and Maryanne Gooze, pp 86–101. Westport, CT: Greenwood, 1995.

Porter, Susan. "'The Imaginative Space' of Medbh McGuckian." *Canadian Journal of Irish Studies* 15, 2 (1989): 93–104.

Sirr, Peter. "'How Things Begin to Happen': Notes on Eiléan Ní Chuilleanáin and Medbh McGuckian." *The Southern Review* 31, 3 (Summer 1995). 450–467.

Wills, Clair. "The Perfect Mother: Authority in the Poetry of Medbh McGuckian." *Text and Context* 3 (Autumn 1988): 91–111.

———. "Voices from the Nursery: Medbh McGuckian's Plantation." *Poetry in Contemporary Irish Literature.* Edited by Michael Kenneally, pp. 373–394. Gerrard's Cross: Colin Smythe, 1995.

———. *Improprieties: Politics and Sexuality in Northern Irish Poetry.* Oxford: Clarendon Press, 1993.

Nuala Ní Dhomhnaill

VOLUMES OF POETRY

An Dealg Droighin. Cork: The Mercier Press, 1981

Féar Suaithinseach. Ma Nuat (Maynooth): An Sagart, 1984.

Rogha Danta / Selected Poems. Translated by Michael Hartnett and
   Nuala Ní Dhomhnaill. Dublin: Raven Arts Press, 1986.

Pharaoh's Daughter. Translated by Ciaran Carson et al. Oldcastle, Co.
   Meath: Gallery Press; Winston-Salem, N.C.: Wake Forest
   University Press, 1990.

The Astrakhan Cloak. Translated by Paul Muldoon. Oldcastle, Co.
   Meath: Gallery Press; Winston-Salem, N.C.: Wake Forest
   University Press, 1993.

Cead Aighnis. An Daingean: An Sagart, 1998.

The Water Horse. Translated by Medbh McGuckian and Eiléan Ní
   Chuilleanáin. Oldcastle Co. Meath: Gallery Press, 1999;
   Winston-Salem, N.C.: Wake Forest University Press, upcoming.

OTHER WORKS BY NÍ DHOMHNAILL

Jimín. Dublin: Deilt Productions, 1985. (play for children)

An Ollphiast Ghránna. Dublin: Deilt Productions, 1987. (play for
   children)

"Making the Millenium: Nuala Ní Dhomhnaill in Conversation
   with Michael Cronin." Dublin: Graph, I 1986.

An Goban Saor. Ilanna Productions, 1993. (screenplay)

An T-Anam Mothala / The Feeling Soul: Ocean Productions, RTE, 1994.
   (screenplay)

Destination Demain. Paris: GES, 1993. (play for children)

The Wooing of Éadoin. National Chambre Choir, 1994. (libretto)

"Comhra, with a Foreward and Afterward by Laura O'Connor." *The
   Southern Review* 31, 3, Summer 1995, pp. 581–614.

'Jumping off Shadows': Selected Contemporary Irish Poets. Edited by Nuala
   Ní Dhomhnaill and Greg Delanty, preface by Philip O'Leary.
   Cork: Cork University Press, 1995.

"Why I Choose to Write in Irish, The Corpse That Sits Up and Talks
   Back." *The New York Times Book Review* (January 8, 1995): 26–28.

"What Foremothers?" *The Comic Tradition in Irish Women Writers.* Edited
   by T. O'Connor, pp. 8–10. Gainesville: University of Florida
   Press, 1996.

"The Hidden Ireland: Women's Inheritance." *Irish Poetry since
   Kavanagh.* Edited by Theo Dorgan. Blackrock, Co. Dublin: Four
   Courts Press, 1996.

"Introduction." *Voices in the Wind: Women Poets of the Celtic Twilight*. Eilís Nic Dhuibhne, ed. Dublin: New Island Books, 1995.

INTERVIEWS

Consalvo, Deborah McWilliams. "An Interview with Nuala Ní Dhomhnaill." *Studies* 83: 331 (Autumn 1994): 313–320.

McDiarmid, Lucy and Michael Durkan. "Q & A: Nuala Ní Dhomhnaill." *Irish Literary Supplement* 6, 2 (Fall 1987): 41–43.

Wilson, Rebecca E. "An Interview with Nuala Ní Dhomhnaill." *Sleeping With Monsters: Conversations with Scottish and Irish Women Poets*. Edited by Rebecca Wilson and Gillean Somerville-Arjat, pp. 148–157. Dublin: Wolfhound Press, 1990.

CRITICISM ON NÍ DHOMHNAILL

Bourke, Angela. "Fairies and Anorexia: Nuala Ní Dhomhnaill's 'Amazing Grass.'" *Proceedings of the Harvard Celtic Colloquium* 13 (1993): 25–38.

Cannon, M. Louise. "The Extraordinary Within the Ordinary: The Poetry of Eavan Boland and Nuala Ní Dhomhnaill.' *South Atlantic Review* 60: 2: 31–46.

Consalvo, Deborah McWilliams. "Nuala Ní Dhomhnaill: Adaptations and Transformations A Second Glance: Bilingualism in Twentieth Century Ireland." *Studies* 83: 331 (Autumn 1994): 303–312.

———. "The Lingual Ideal in the Poetry of Nuala Ní Dhomhnaill." *Eire-Ireland* 30, 2 (Summer 1995): 148–161.

———. "Nuala Ní Dhomhnaill." *Modern Irish Writers: A Bio-Critical Sourcebook*. Edited by Alexander Gonzalez, pp. 278–282. London: Aldwych Press, 1997.

Haberstroh, Patricia Boyle. "Nuala Ní Dhomhnaill." *Women Creating Women*, pp. 161–195. Syracuse: Syracuse University Press, 1996.

Mac Giolla Leith, Caoimhin. "Contemporary Poetry in Irish: Private Language and Ancestral Voices." *Poetry in Contemporary Irish Literature*. Edited by Michael Kenneally, pp. 84–98. Gerrard's Cross: Colin Smythe.

Murphy, Maureen. "The Irish Elegiac Tradition in the Poetry of Maire Mhac an tSaoi, Caitlin Maude, and Nuala Ní Dhomhnaill." *New Irish Writing*. Edited by James Brophy and Eamon Grennan, pp. 141–151. Boston: GK Hall, 1989.

———. "Folklore in the Poetry of Nuala Ní Dhomhnaill." *International Aspects of Irish Literature*. Edited by Toshi Furomoto, George Hughes, Chizuko Inoue, James McElwaine, Peter

McMillan, and Tetsuro Sano, pp. 14–23. Gerrard's Cross: Colin Smythe, 1996.

O'Connor, Mary. "Lashings of the Mother Tongue: Nuala Ní Dhomhnaill's Anarchic Laughter." *The Comic Tradition in Irish Women Writers*. Edited by Theresa O'Connor, pp. 149–170. Gainesville, La: University of Florida Press, 1996.

Ó Tuama, Seán. "'The Loving and Terrible Mother' in the Early Poetry of Nuala Ní Dhomhnaill." *Repossessions: Selected Essays on the Irish Literary Heritage*, pp. 35–53. Cork: Cork University Press, 1995.

Revie, Linda. "The Little Red Fox, Emblem of the Irish Peasant in Poems by Yeats, Tynan and Ní Dhomhnaill." *Learning the Trade: Essays on W.B. Yeats and Contemporary Poetry*. Edited by Deborah Fleming, pp. 113–133. West Cornwall, CT: Locust Hill, 1993.

———. "Nuala Ní Dhomhnaill's 'Parthenogenesis': A Bisexual Exchange." *Poetry in Contemporary Irish Literature*. Edited by Michael Kenneally, pp. 344–355. Gerrard's Cross: Colin Smythe, 1995.

Rita Ann Higgins

VOLUMES OF POETRY

Goddess on the Mervue Bus. Galway: Salmon, 1986.

Witch in the Bushes. Galway: Salmon, 1988.

Goddess and Witch. Galway: Salmon, 1990.

Philomena's Revenge. Galway: Salmon, 1992.

Higher Purchase. Co. Clare: Salmon, 1996.

Sunnyside Plucked: New and Selected Poems, Newcastle upon Tyne: Bloodaxe, 1996.

CRITICISM ON HIGGINS

Steele, Karen. "Refusing the Poisoned Chalice: The Sexual Politics of Rita Ann Higgins and Paula Meehan." *Homemaking: Women Writers and the Politics and Poetics of Home*. Edited by Catherine Wiley and Fiona Barnes, pp. 312–333. New York: Garland, 1996.

Paula Meehan

VOLUMES OF POETRY

Return and No Blame. Donnybrook: Beaver Row, 1984.

Reading the Sky. Donnybrook: Beaver Row, 1986.

The Man Who Was Marked by Winter. Oldcastle, Co. Meath: Gallery
    Press, 1991; Cheney, WA: Eastern Washington University
    Press, 1994.
Pillow Talk, Oldcastle, Co. Meath: Gallery Press, 1994.
Mysteries of the Home: Selected Poems. Newcastle Upon Tyne: Bloodaxe
    Books, 1996.

INTERVIEWS
Dorgan, Theo. "An Interview with Paula Meehan." *Colby Quarterly*
    28, 4 (Dec 1992): 265–269.

CRITICISM ON MEEHAN
Steele, Karen. "Refusing the Poisoned Chalice: The Sexual Politics
    of Rita Ann Higgins and Paula Meehan." *Homemaking: Women
    Writers and the Politics and Poetics of Home.* Edited by Catherine
    Wiley and Fiona Barnes, pp. 312–333. New York: Garland, 1996.

Moya Cannon

VOLUMES OF POETRY
Oar. Galway: Salmon, 1990.
The Parchment Boat. Oldcastle, Co. Meath: Gallery Press, 1997.

OTHER WORKS BY CANNON
Cúm: An Anthology of New Writing from Co. Kerry. Edited by Moya
    Cannon. Co. Kerry: Kerry Co. Council, 1996.

Mary O'Malley

VOLUMES OF POETRY
A Consideration of Silk. Galway: Salmon Publishing, 1990.
Where the Rocks Float. Galway: Salmon, 1993.
The Knife in the Wave. Co Clare: Salmon, 1997.

Kerry Hardie

VOLUMES OF POETRY
A Furious Place. Oldcastle, Co. Meath: Gallery Press, 1996.

Criticism

ON IRISH WOMEN'S POETRY

Archer, Nuala, ed. "Women Alone." *Midland Review* 3, 50 (1986) (special issue on Irish women writers).

Bradley, Anthony and Maryann Gialanella Valiulis. *Gender and Sexuality in Modern Ireland.* Amherst: University of Massachusetts Press, 1997.

Brophy, James D. and Eamon Grennan, eds. *New Irish Writing.* Boston: GK Hall, 1989.

Clifton, Harry. "Real and Synthetic Whiskey: A Generation of Irish Poets, 1975–1987." *New Irish Writing.* Edited by James D. Brophy and Eamon Grennan, pp. 232–247. Boston: GK Hall, 1989.

Curtin, Chris; Pauline Jackson; and Barbara O'Connor, eds. *Gender in Irish Society.* Galway: Galway University Press, 1987.

Donovan, Katie. *Irish Women Writers: Marginalized by Whom?* Dublin: Raven Arts, 1988.

Haberstroh, Patricia Boyle. "Literary Politics: Mainstream and Margin." *Canadian Journal of Irish Studies* 18, 1 (1992): 181–91.

———. *Women Creating Women: Contemporary Irish Women Poets.* Syracuse: Syracuse University Press, 1996.

Hannon, Dennis J. and Nancy Means Wright. "Irish Women Poets: Breaking the Silence." *Canadian Journal of Irish Studies* 16, 2 (1990): 57–65.

Henigan, Robert. "Contemporary Women Poets in Ireland." *Concerning Poetry* 18, 1–2 (1985): 103–115.

Johnston, Dillon. *Irish Poetry After Joyce.* South Bend, Indiana: Notre Dame University Press, 1985; 2d ed., rev. Syracuse: Syracuse University Press, 1997.

Johnson, Toni O'Brien and David Cairns. *Gender in Irish Writing.* Milton Keynes and Philadelphia: Open University Press, 1991.

Luftig, Victor. "A Migrant Mind in a Mobile Home: Salmon Publishing in the Ireland of the 1990's." *Eire-Ireland* 26, 1 (1989): 108–119.

McElroy, James. "Night Feed: An Overview of Ireland's Women Poets." *American Poetry Review* (January/February 1985): 32–36.

———. "The Contemporary Fe/Male Poet: A Preliminary Reading." *New Irish Writing.* Edited by James D. Brophy and Eamon Grennan, pp. 197–220. Boston: GK Hall, 1989.

McGuinness, Arthur. "Hearth and History: Poetry by Contemporary Irish Women." *Cultural Contexts and Literary Idioms in Contemporary Irish Literature.* Edited by Michael Kenneally, pp. 97–220. Totowa, NJ: Barnes and Noble.

Meaney, Geraldine. "History Gasps: Myth in Contemporary Irish Women's Poetry." *Poetry in Contemporary Irish Literature.* Edited by Michael Kenneally, pp. 99–113. Gerrard's Cross: Colin Smythe, 1995.

Murphy, Maureen. "The Irish Elegiac Tradition in the Poetry of Maire Mhac an tSaoi, Caitlin Maude, and Nuala Ní Dhomhnaill." *New Irish Writing.* Edited by James Brophy and Eamon Grennan, pp. 141–151. Boston: GK Hall, 1989.

Somerville-Arjat, Gillean and Rebecca E. Wilson, Editors. *Sleeping with Monsters: Conversations with Scottish and Irish Women Poets.* Dublin: Wolfhound, 1990.

Weekes, Ann Owens. *Irish Women Writers: An Uncharted Tradition.* Lexington: University of Kentucky Press, 1990.

———. *Unveiling Treasures: The Attic Guide to the Published Works of Irish Women Literary Writers.* Dublin: Attic, 1993.

ON IRISH WOMEN'S CULTURE

Beale, Jenny. *Women in Ireland: Voices of Change.* Basingstoke: Macmillan, 1986.

Brady, Anne M. *Women in Ireland: An Annotated Bibliography.* Westport, Conn.: Greenwood, 1988.

Coulter, Carol. "'Hello Divorce, Goodbye Daddy': Women, Gender, and the Divorce Debate." *Gender and Sexuality in Modern Ireland.* Edited by Anthony Bradley and Maryann Gialanella Valiulis, pp. 275–298. Amherst: University of Massachusetts Press, 1997.

Herr, Cheryl. "The Erotics of Irishness." *Critical Inquiry* 17: (1990): 1–34.

Innes, L. *Women and Nation in Irish Literature.* London: Harvester, 1993.

Longley, Edna. "From Cathleen to Anorexia: The Breakdown of Irelands." Dublin: Attic Press LIP Pamphlet, 1990; reprinted in *The Living Stream.* Newcastle Upon Tyne: Bloodaxe, 1994.

Luddy, Maria, and Cliona Murphy. *Women Surviving: Studies in Irish Women's History in the 19th and 20th Centuries.* Swords: Co Dublin, Pollbeg, 1989.

MacCurtain, Margaret. "Godly Burden: The Catholic Sisterhoods in Twentieth-Century Ireland." *Gender and Sexuality in Modern Ireland.* Edited by Anthony Bradley and Maryann Gialanella Valiulis, pp. 245–256. Amherst: University of Massachusetts Press, 1997.

———. "Towards an Appraisal of the Religious Image of Women." *The Crane Bag* 4, 1 (1980): 26–30.

——— and Donncha O Corrain, eds. *Women in Irish Society: The Historical Dimension.* Dublin: Arlen House, 1978.

Meaney, Geraldine. "Sex and Nation, Women in Irish Culture and Politics." Dublin: Attic Press LIP Pamphlet, 1991.

Nulty, Christine. "Images of Irish Women." *Crane Bag Book of Irish Studies*. Edited by Richard Kearney and Mark Patrick Hederman. Dublin: Blackwater, 1982.

O'Dowd, Mary, and Maryann Gialanella Valiulis, eds. *Women in Irish History*. Dublin: Wolfhound, 1997.

Sailer, Susan Shaw. *Representing Ireland: Gender, Class, Nationality*. Gainesville: University of Florida Press, 1997.

Scannell, Yvonne. "The Constitution and the Role of Women." *De Valera's Constitution and Ours*. Edited by Brian Farrell, pp 123–136. Dublin: Gill and Macmillan, 1988.

Shannon, Catherine. "The Changing Face of Cathleen Ní Houlihan: Women and Politics in Ireland, 1960–66." *Gender and Sexuality in Modern Ireland*. Edited by Anthony Bradley and Maryann Gialanella Valiulis, pp. 257–274. Amherst: University of Massachusetts Press, 1997.

Smyth, Ailbhe. "The Floozie in the Jacuzzi," *The Irish Review 6* (Spring 1989): 7–24.

———. "Women and Power in Ireland: Problems, Progress, Practice." *Women's Studies International Forum 8.4* (1985): 255–262.

———. *Women's Rights in Ireland*. Dublin: Ward River Press, 1983.

ON GAELIC IRISH TRADITION

Alison, Jonathan. "Poetry from the Irish." *Irish Literary Supplement 10*, 1 (1991): 14.

Bourke, Angela. "More in Anger than in Sorrow: Irish Women's Lament Poetry." *Feminist Messages*. Edited by Joan Newlon Radner, pp. 160–182. Urbana: University of Illinois Press, 1993.

———. "Performing–not Writing." *Graph 11* (1991–1992): 28–31.

———. "The Virtual Reality of Irish Fairy Legend." *Eire- Ireland 31*, 1&2 (1996): 7–25.

———. "Working and Weeping: Women's Oral Poetry in Irish and Scottish Gaelic Poetry." *Women's Studies Working Papers*. Dublin: UCD Women's Studies Forum, 1988.

Caldecott, Moyra. *Women in Celtic Myth*. Rochester, Vt.: Destiny Books, 1988.

Clark, Rosalind. *The Great Queens: Irish Goddesses from the Mórrigan to Cathleen Ní Houlihan*. Gerrard's Cross: Colin Smythe, 1991.

Condren, Mary. *The Serpent and the Goddess: Women, Religion and Power in Celtic Ireland*. New York: Harper and Row, 1989.

Henry, P.L., ed. *Dánta Ban: Poems of Irish Women, Early and Modern.* Dublin: Mercier, 1990.

Kiberd, Declan and Gabriel Fitzmaurice, eds. *An Crann Faoi Bláth: The Flowering Tree: Contemporary Irish Poetry with Verse Translations.* Dublin: Wolfhound Press, 1991.

Kinsella, Thomas and Seán Ó'Tuama. *An Duanaire 1600-1900: Poems of the Dispossessed.* Dublin: The Dolmen Press, 1981.

Kinsella, Thomas. *The Dual Tradition: An Essay on Poetry and Politics in Ireland.* Manchester: Carcanet, 1995.

Lysaght, Patricia. *The Banshee: The Irish Supernatural Death Messenger.* Dublin: Glendale Press, 1986.

MacCurtain, Margaret and Mary O'Dowd, eds. *Women in Early Modern Ireland.* Edinburgh: Edinburgh University Press, 1991.

Mhac an tSaoi, Maire. "The Female Principle in Gaelic Poetry." *Women in Irish Life and Legend.* Edited by S.F. Gallagher, pp. 26–38. Totowa, NJ: Barnes and Noble, 1983.

Murphy, Gerard. "Notes on Aisling Poetry." *Éigse* 1, 1 (1939): 40–50.

O'Donoghue, Bernard. "The Translator's Voice, Irish Poetry before Yeats." *Princeton University Library Chronicle* 59, 3 (Spring 1998): 298–320.

O'Rourke, Brian. "The Long Walk of a Queen: The Representation of Ireland as a Woman in the Irish Literary Tradition." *Chiba Review* 7 (1985): 1–49.

Wood, Helen Lanigan. Women in Myths and Early Depictions." *Irish Women: Image and Achievement.* Edited by Eiléan Ní Chuilleanáin. Dublin: Arlen House, 1985.

ON CONTEMPORARY IRISH POETRY

Andrews, Elmer, ed. *Contemporary Irish Poetry: A Collection of Critical Essays.* London: Macmillan, 1990.

Bedient, Calvin. "The Crabbed Genius of Belfast." *Parnassus: Poetry in Review* 16, no. 1: 195–210.

Bradley, Anthony. "The Irishness of Irish Poetry after Years." *New Irish Writing.* Edited by James D. Brophy and Eamon Grennan. Boston: G.K. Hall, 1989.

Corcoran, Neil. *The Chosen Ground: Essays on the Contemporary Poetry of Northern Ireland.* Chester Springs, PA: Dufour, 1992.

———. *After Yeats and Joyce: Reading Modern Irish Literature.* Oxford: Oxford University Press, 1997.

Fallon, Peter. "Notes on a History of Publishing Poetry." *Princeton University Library Chronicle* 59, 3 (Spring 1998): 546–58.

Garrett, Robert F. "The Place of Writing and the Writing of Place in

Twentieth-Century Irish Poetry in English." *Poetry in the British Isles: Non-Metropolitan Perspectives*. Edited by Hans Werner Ludwig et al, pp. 173–92. Swansea: University of Wales Press, 1995.

Johnston, Dillon. *Irish Poetry After Joyce*. South Bend, Indiana: Notre Dame University Press, 1985; 2d ed., rev., Syracuse: Syracuse University Press, 1997.

———. "Next to Nothing: Uses of the Otherworld in Modern Irish Literature." *New Irish Writing*. Edited by James Brophy and Eamon Grennan. Boston: G.K. Hall, 1989.

———. "Wake Forest University Press: Some Reflections." *Princeton University Library Chronicle* 59, 3 (Spring 1998): 581–93.

Longley, Edna. "An ABC of Reading Contemporary Irish Poetry." *Princeton University Library Chronicle* 59, 3 (Spring 1998): 517–45.

———. *Poetry in the Wars*. Newcastle Upon Tyne: Bloodaxe, 1986.

Mahony, Christina Hunt. "Poetry in Modern Ireland–Where Post-Colonial and Post-Modern Part Ways." *The Comparatist* (Spring, 1996): 89–92.

———. *Contemporary Irish Literature: Transforming Tradition*. New York: St. Martin's Press, 1998.

McDonald, Peter. "Yeats, Form and Northern Irish Poetry." *Yeats Annual* 12, (1996): 13–42.

———. *Mistaken Identities: Poetry and Northern Ireland*. Oxford: Clarendon Press, 1997.

Muldoon, Paul. "The Point of Poetry." *Princeton University Library Chronicle* 59, 3 (Spring 1998): 503–16.

Stevens, Matthew. *Irish Poetry: Politics, History, Negotiation, the Evolving Debate, 1969 to the Present*. New York: St. Martins, 1997.

Wills, Clair. "Modes of Redress: the Elegy in Recent Irish Poetry." *Princeton University Library Chronicle* 59, 3 (Spring 1998): 594–620.

GENERAL REFERENCE WORKS

Deane, Seamus, ed. *The Field Day Anthology of Irish Writing*. Derry: Field Day Publications, 1991.

Hogan, Robert. *The Dictionary of Irish Literature* (revised and updated second edition, two-volume set). London: Aldwych Press, 1997.

Share, Bernard. *Slanguage: A Dictionary of Slang and Colloquial English in Ireland*. Dublin: Gill and Macmillan, 1997.

Smyth, Ailbhe, Editor. *Wildish Things: An Anthology of New Irish Women's Writing*. Dublin: Attic Press, 1989.

Permissions

The editors gratefully acknowledge the permission of these writers and publishers to reprint the material in this book:

Eavan Boland

Poems from *New Territory, In Her Own Image, Night Feed,* and *The Journey* reprinted from *An Origin Like Water: Collected Poems 1967–1987* and from *Outside History, In a Time of Violence,* and *The Lost Land* with the permission of W.W. Norton & Co.

Eiléan Ní Chuilleanáin

Poems from *The Second Voyage, The Magdalene Sermon and Earlier Poems, The Brazen Serpent,* and the poems "The Girl Who Married the Reindeer," "Bessboro," "Translation (for the reburial of the Magdalens)," and "Alcove" reprinted with the permission of The Gallery Press.

Medbh McGuckian

Poems from *The Flower Master* and *Venus and the Rain* reprinted with the permission of The Gallery Press. Poems from *On Ballycastle Beach, Marconi's Cottage, Captain Lavender,* and *Shelmalier* reprinted with the permission of Wake Forest University Press.

Nuala Ní Dhomhnaill

Poems and translations from *Selected Poems* reprinted with the permission of the Author and of the Translator, Michael Hartnett. Poems and translations from *Pharaoh's Daughter,* poems from *The Astrakhan Cloak,* and the poems and translations "Tusa" / "You Are," "An tEach Uisce" / "The Water-Horse," "An Mhuruch san Ospideal" / "The Mermaid in the Labour Ward," and "Na Murucha Ag Ni a gCeann" / "The Marianne Faithful Hairdo" reprinted with the permission of The Gallery Press. Translations from *The Astrakhan Cloak* reprinted with permission of the Translator, Paul Muldoon.

Rita Ann Higgins

Poems from *Goddess on the Mervue Bus, Witch in the Bushes, Philomena's Revenge*, and *Higher Purchase* reprinted with the permission of Salmon Publishing Ltd.

Paula Meehan

Poems from *The Man Who Was Marked by Winter* and *Pillow Talk* reprinted with the permission of The Gallery Press.

Moya Cannon

Poems from *Oar* reprinted with the permission of Salmon Publishing Ltd. Poems from *The Parchment Boat* reprinted with the permission of The Gallery Press.

Mary O'Malley

Poems from *Where the Rocks Float* and *The Knife in the Wave* reprinted with the permission of Salmon Publishing Ltd.

Kerry Hardie

Poems from *A Furious Place* reprinted with the permission of The Gallery Press.

Index of titles

309